EVERYDAY CREATIVITY

An Easy to Read Guide

by Kathy Goff, EdD

FOREWORD by
E. Paul Torrance, PhD
Distinguished Professor Emeritus

Little Ox Books

Copyright © by Kathy Goff 1998

ISBN 0-9657491-1-8

Library of Congress Catalog Number: 98-065465

Published by Little Ox Books
3824 N. Airport Lane
Stillwater, OK 74075
Phone: 405-372-0810
Fax: 405-377-5284
E-mail: mcgoff@cowboy.net

PREFACE

I was very fortunate that E. Paul Torrance wrote the Foreword for this book. He is a world renowned author, educator and researcher in the field of creativity. He has studied the elusive human characteristic of creativity for over 50 years. His creativity tests are standardized in numerous countries. He has been a very prolific writer with over 1200 articles and 40 books on the subject.

It was one of his books, *The Search for Satori and Creativity* that captured my attention. When I read this book, it was as if someone was speaking my language. I felt a kindred spirit was writing this book, so I went to the University of Georgia to get my doctorate and learn from E. Paul Torrance. Within two weeks of arriving in Athens, Georgia, Dr. Torrance, retired and working in his home, hired me to be his research assistant. I worked side by side with him daily for 4 years.

It's been over ten years since we met. We correspond through the mail weekly as we have done for more than six years. He is my mentor, my colleague and my good friend. I call him "Ghandi II" because he is brilliant, peaceful, kind and gentle. E. Paul Torrance is a man whose work and life have changed the world for the better.

K. G.

FOREWORD

Marilyn Vos Savant who reputedly has the highest Intelligence Quotient (IQ) ever recorded was asked (*Parade Magazine*, February, 1997) why educators believe that intelligence can be measured. Her reply was:

>Because such as measure would be so useful...Speaking for myself, I think trying to measure intelligence is like trying to measure beauty. Most of use will agree that some people are more attractive than others, but there are *many* different kinds of wonderful.

The same might be said of creativity that Marilyn Vos Savant said of intelligence and beauty. Scholars have long recognized that there are numerous kinds of intelligence. However, they had not clearly identified them until Howard Gardner came along with his theory of multiple intelligences. He identified seven kinds of intelligences or pathways to learning. Although Gardner identified seven kinds of intelligences, he has not offered a plan for measuring them. However, he has captured the imagination of educators and his seven intelligences are being used as "pathways to learning." The pathways are:
1. Linguistic intelligence (as a poet or other type of writer or speaker);
2. Logical-mathematical intelligence (as in a scientist);

3. Musical intelligence (as a composer);
4. Spatial intelligence (as in a sculptor or airplane pilot);
5. Bodily-kinesthetic intelligence (as in an athlete or dancer);
6. Interpersonal intelligence (as in a salesman or teacher);
7. Intrapersonal intelligence (exhibited by individuals with accurate views of themselves).

It would be possible to think of creativity in the same way. However, creativity scholars and practitioners have not made any move in this direction. However, they have recognized that there are many ways of being creative but we do not yet know what is the best way to conceptualize them. Kathy Goff, in this book, emphasizes what I have called "every-day creativity." She rightly believes that all individuals are creative and that their creativity can be enhanced or blocked in many ways. She agrees with me that anytime people are confronted with situations for which they have not already learned and practiced a response, some degree or kind of creativity is required.

The author is also unique in considering creativity developmentally. Creativity scholars and writers have not done this. There are many reasons for this. Perhaps the most important is that so many people have mistakenly thought that the level of a person's creativity was established at an early age (at age two or three). There is much evidence that this is not true. However, research has demonstrated that creativity does not always develop linearly. Many factors may throw it off course—pressures to conformity, environment, teaching methods, and the like. The author of this book rightly contends that it is possible to use activities, teaching methods, motivation and procedures to produce growth, even in aging.

Other unique features not usually found in texts on creativity are chapters on mentoring, humor and inventing. It has been shown that having a mentor makes a significant difference in creative achievement. There has already been some recognition that humor facilitates creativity, but it has generally been rather silent. The author's personal experience as an inventor has equipped her to write on this aspect of creativity.

This book is written in an easy to read style and will be especially favored by parents, teachers, the elderly, business people, and other groups not specialized in creativity research. Rarely have the elderly been considered in creativity texts.

                      E. Paul Torrance
                      Georgia Studies of Creative Behavior
                      Athens, Georgia

INTRODUCTION

I wrote this book to pass along what I have learned. I believe that our everyday creativity is the key to a healthy, happy, satisfying life. Tapping into my creativity has saved my life and has saved the lives of many people. Creativity is a life force within us all as human beings. It can be developed at any age in an infinite number of ways and only ceases to develop when we do. Everyday creativity is the ability to see a situation in many ways and to continue to question until satisfaction is reached.

Many times our everyday creativity is being developed without our even knowing it. For example, when I travel with my business partner, we come up with some our best and most creative ideas and inventions. Developing our creativity is the furthest thing from our mind, but that is exactly what we are doing. By getting away from the everyday duties and responsibilities, our minds are free to create and imagine possibilities. As you learn more about your own thinking styles and your creativity, you will learn what encourages it and what kind of environment you need to be the most creative.

A key ingredient in any partnership is utilizing each other's strengths. It is important to know who does what best and to let them contribute those skills or abilities. We must learn the skills of interdependence in order to achieve productive, healthy, happy, self-actualizing lives.

We must be much better investigators, before we begin labeling children at younger and younger ages, with back breaking yokes of negative baggage. We must identify their strengths and teach them how to develop and utilize those strengths instead of constantly remediating their "weaknesses." This is not to say that we should only look for the positive, but we need to look at the positives of life with as much vigor as we have used and continue to use to examine the negatives of life.

We must be much more determined to identify the strengths of our children, youth, adults and elders and support their successes and achievements in order to make our lives better. All of us can be better caretakers of our world and our lives. I hope this book will be of some assistance to you in tapping and enhancing your everyday creativity and the everyday creativity of others. Peace.

    Kathy Goff
    McGoff Creative Enterprises
    Stillwater, OK

TABLE OF CONTENTS

Chapter 1: Creativity and E. Paul Torrance 1

Chapter 2: Creative Abilities 11

Chapter 3: Learning and Children 25

Chapter 4: Creative Learning and Incubation . . 43

Chapter 5: Creativity and Personal Strengths . . 49

Chapter 6: Creative Problem Solving 63

Chapter 7: Creativity, Play and the Arts 73

Chapter 8: Creativity, Humor and Wellness . . . 81

Chapter 9: Inventing and Futuristics 93

Chapter 10: Creativity and Mentoring 115

Chapter 11: Lifelong Creativity 127

Chapter 12: Creativity Tips 137

Appendix A: Ideas for Activities 147

Appendix B: Sample Incubation Model
    Activities 151

References 157

Subject Index 169

Everyday Creativity: An Easty-to-Read Guide

Chapter 1
CREATIVITY AND E. PAUL TORRANCE

Creative thinking is much more than using our imaginations to invent lots of new ideas. Creative thinking is a lifestyle, a personality trait, a way of looking at the world, a way of interacting with others and a way of living and growing. Living creatively means developing our talents, tapping our unused potentials and becoming what we are capable of becoming through self-discovery and self-discipline. Anytime we are faced with a problem or dilemma with no learned or practiced solution, some creativity is required (Torrance, 1962; 1988).

Creativity is a vital ingredient in meeting the challenges of a continuous life cycle, a cycle in which growth and change are the norm from conception throughout life. A life filled with growth and change requires a conscious effort to think creatively. To develop creativeness, the mind needs to be exercised as well as filled with materials out of which ideas can be formed. The richest fuel for ideation is firsthand experience (Osborn, 1963).

Creativity Research

Generally there are four major perspectives in creativity research: creative product, creative environment, creative personality and creative process. As you would imagine, the creative product research has focused on the tangible, on something concrete that was original and had some value, usefulness or social acceptance. Creative products include works of art, scientific discoveries, solutions to problems, inventions, consumer goods, adaptations, etc.

The creative environment research has focused on whether supportive, structured environments, or unstructured, permissive environments encouraged creativity. Generally, it is agreed that creativity is enhanced through providing environmental conditions that encourage its functioning and development. Hot, stuffy, small rooms are not as conductive to learning and creative expressions as open, well lighted and ventilated spaces. The actual physical environment influences creativity and learning.

The creative personality research was initiated by Freud (1910) who suggested that creativity was a substitute for achieving satisfactions and was therefore an escape from the hardships of reality. On the other hand, some psychologists viewed the creative impulse as stemming from one's essential health, that creativity appeared to be the same as one's tendency to actualize him/herself. Creativity has been described as the most basic manifestation of a man or woman fulfilling his/her own being in the world.

The creative process research has examined how creative solutions or products were formulated. In 1926, Wallas suggested four stages in forming a new thought: preparation, incubation, illumination and verification. Torrance defines creativity as the process of sensing problems or gaps in information, forming ideas or hypotheses, testing and modifying these hypotheses, and communicating the results. I define creativity as the ability to see a situation in many ways and to continue to question until satisfaction is reached.

The creative process can involve tiny creative leaps or giant breakthroughs in thinking. Both require that an individual go beyond where they have gone before, embracing the unknown, the mysterious, the change, the puzzling without fear. It takes courage to be creative.

The creative process may be considered as a new way of seeing, a different point of view, an original idea or a new relationship between ideas. It is the way or manner in which a problem is solved. It is the process of bringing something new into being. It is the process of combining previously unrelated ideas or perceiving a new relationship from previously unrelated ideas.

E. Paul Torrance

E. Paul Torrance has been a pioneer in creativity research and education for more than 50 years. He is a monumental figure who has helped make a better world through his lifetime focus on the development of creative potential of individuals of all abilities and ages. He has produced over 1800 publications and presentations on creativity (Millar, 1997).

Torrance chose to define creativity as a process because he thought if we understood the creative process, we could predict what kind of person could master the process, what kind of climate made it grow and what products would be involved (Torrance, 1995a). Torrance created a battery of tests of creative thinking abilities for use from kindergarten through graduate and professional education. The *Torrance Tests of Creative Thinking (TTCT)* are the most widely used tests of creative talent in the United States and have been translated into over 30 different languages. The *TTCT* have been standardized and published in France, Italy and China. There is very little racial, socioeconomic or cultural bias in the *TTCT* (Torrance, 1988).

In longitudinal studies (1958-1980), Torrance found that students identified as creatively gifted, but not intellectually gifted (IQ of 130+), out achieved the intellectually, but not creatively gifted, in adulthood. He has found that characteristics of the creative thinking abilities differ from those of the abilities involved in intelligence and logical reasoning. In fact, the use of intelligence tests to identify gifted students misses about 70% of those who are equally gifted on creativity criteria, such as the *TTCT* (Torrance, 1988).

Torrance has found that having a mentor who helps in learning how to "play one's own game" is significantly related to adult creative achievement. A major function of mentors seems to be helping the protege/student to learn to use their best abilities and doing the things they "love" - following their dreams. He also found that having a childhood future career image ("being in love with something") and persisting with it is related significantly to adult creative achievement and living. According to Torrance (1995a, p. 13), one of the most powerful wellsprings of creative energy, outstanding accomplishment and self-fulfillment seems to be falling in love with something - your dream, your image of the future.

Torrance's research has demonstrated that a variety of techniques for training in creative problem solving produce significant creative growth without interfering with traditional kinds of educational achievement. Creative growth seems to be greatest and most predictable when deliberate, direct teaching of creative thinking skills is involved. Torrance believes that each person is unique and has particular strengths that are of value and must be respected. Therefore education must be built upon strengths rather than weaknesses.

Dr. Torrance shared this experiment with me and I found it to be very pertinent to educating young children. The experiment with a single litter of rats demonstrates the power of learned behaviors as a result of sensory deprivation. The litter was divided into three groups. The ears of one group were taped, they eyes of another were taped, and the third group was left alone. In time, the taped groups learned to adapt to their deafness and blindness. The tape was then removed and they learned to adjust as hearing and seeing rats. However, under stress, those who had been taped reverted to the deaf and blind behaviors. So if children learn to suppress or neglect their creative potential, then when faced with stress as adults, we will most likely not refer to or rely on our creative abilities to deal with stresses. We will revert back to learned defensive behaviors instead of opening up to new possibilites and options.

Torrance saw that it takes courage to be creative. Just as soon as you have a new idea, you are a minority of one. Torrance (1979) found that learning and thinking creatively takes place in the processes of sensing difficulties, problems, gaps in information; in making guesses or formulating hypotheses about these deficiencies; in testing these guesses and possibly revising and retesting them; and finally in communicating the results. Vital human needs are involved in each of these four stages. If we sense that something is missing or wrong, tension is aroused, we are uncomfortable, and to relieve our tension we try to make guesses in order to fill gaps and make connections. We know that our guesses may be wrong, but we find out early on if they are correct or not. Thus we are driven to test our hypotheses, to modify them, to correct our errors. Once we make a discovery, we want to tell somebody about it. This is one reason why it is so natural for humans to learn creatively.

I first became acquainted with Torrance's work in 1984 in an extension course during my masters program in gifted education. I took a "Creativity for Teachers" course and Torrance's book *The Search for Satori and Creativity* was the text. I was hooked. I did my masters thesis on creativity and went to the University of Georgia to study creativity at the Torrance Center for Creative Studies in 1987.

Upon arriving in Athens, I found that Dr. Torrance was retired and working out of his home. I met him and he offered me a job evaluating *Sounds and Images* protocols from Arkansas students. I jumped at the opportunity and began work the day after he asked me. I continued to work for Dr. Torrance as his personal research assistant, in his home for the next 4 years.

Upon completion of my doctorate in 1991, I returned to Oklahoma to teach, train, research and advocate for creativity. Dr. Torrance and I have continued to correspond weekly for the past 7 years. He continues to be my cherished mentor. I would like to conclude with examples of insights Dr. Torrance

(1995b, p. 319-320) has identified as a result of his research.

Insight: Creativity tests, such as the TTCT, are lacking in economic, gender and racial bias, especially if the tests are given early (Torrance, 1977).

Insight: Disadvantaged children may perform better than affluent or gifted students in brainstorming (Torrance, 1977).

Insight: Apparent procrastination may result in greater incubation and creative achievement (Torrance and Safter, 1990).

Insight: The willingness to disagree in a group facilitates creativity and making of better decisions (Torrance, 1957).

Insight: Young children can begin learning negotiation skills (Murdock and Torrance, 1988).

Insight: Creatively gifted children with learning disabilities may attain a high degree of success in a field that he/she loves if his/her strengths are regarded positively (Torrance, 1992).

Insight: Creativity is an infinite phenomenon. A person can be creative in an endless number of ways. The outcomes of creative behavior are inexhaustible. (Torrance, 1971, p. 35)

Dr. Torrance is a tireless advocate for creativity and the creative potentials of all people of all ages and abilities. His "Manifesto for Children," also called "How to Grow Up Creatively Gifted," provides seven key ingredients for being more creative at any age. Dr. Torrance continues to write and conduct research from his home in Athens, GA. He is a good friend to the world and a national treasure. I would like to thank him for all of his work and dedication to the creatively gifted and the nontraditional learner.

If you would like to know more about E. Paul Torrance and his work I would recommend two fairly recent publications:

Torrance, E. P. (1995). *Why fly? A philosophy of creativity*. Norwood, NJ: Ablex Publishing Co.
Millar, G. W. (1995). *E. Paul Torrance - "The Creativity Man:" An authorized biography*. Norwood, NJ: Ablex Publishing Co.

HOW TO GROW UP CREATIVELY GIFTED
by E. Paul Torrance

1. Don't be afraid to "fall in love with" something and pursue it with intensity. (You will do best what you like to do most.)

2. Know, understand, take pride in, practice, develop, use, exploit and enjoy your greatest strengths.

3. Learn to free yourself from the expectations of others and walk away from the games they try to impose upon you.

4. Free yourself to play your own game in such a way as to make good use of your gifts.

5. Find a great teacher or mentor who will help you.

6. Don't waste a lot of expensive, unproductive energy trying to be well-rounded. (Don't try to do everything; do what you can do well and what you love.)

7. Learn the skills of interdependence. (Learn to depend upon one another, giving freely of your greatest strengths and most intense loves.)

Chapter 2
CREATIVE ABILITIES

> Creativity defies precise definition. This conclusion does not bother me at all. In fact, I am quite happy with it. Creativity is almost infinite. It involves every sense - sight, smell, hearing, feeling, taste, and even perhaps the extrasensory. Much of it is unseen, nonverbal, and unconscious. Therefore, even if we had a precise conception of creativity, I am certain we would have difficulty putting it into words. (Torrance, 1988, p. 43)

Torrance began investigating creativity during his work in the U.S. Air Force Survival Training School. During this time he defined creativity as occurring when a person has no learned or practiced solution to a problem and some creativity is required. Torrance spent seven years directing a program of research in support of U.S. Air Force survival training (1951-1957). The air force was training its aircrewmen to survive emergencies and extreme conditions. In survival training, crews were given factual information as well as practice in simulated situations. However, in actual emergency and extreme conditions, the aircrewmen were facing new situations for which they had no learned or practiced solution.

In survival situations, aircrewmen need creative solutions from imaginatively recombining old elements with the new situation. Torrance found that the elements of a creative solution could be taught, but the creativity itself must be self-discovered and self-disciplined. Thus, an important part of the survival training involved practicing means of self-discovery, self-discipline and the use of the imagination (Torrance, 1957a).

Following his work in the Air Force, Torrance began formal research into creativity at the University of Minnesota. His primary method for learning about the nature of creativity has been through testing and teaching creative behavior. For research purposes, Torrance chose a process definition of creativity. Torrance believed that if he chose the creative process as a focus, he could then ask what kind of person engages in the process successfully, what kinds of environments facilitate it, and what kinds of products result from successful use of the process (Torrance, 1965a).

Torrance (1988, p. 47) defines creative thinking as a process of sensing difficulties, problems, gaps in information, missing elements, something askew; making guesses and formulating hypotheses about these deficiencies; evaluating and testing these guesses and hypotheses; possibly revising and retesting them; and finally communicating the results.

According to Torrance (1988) strong human needs appear to be at the basis of each of its stages. If we sense an incompleteness, something missing or out of place, tension is aroused. Consequently, we begin investigating, asking questions, manipulating things, making guesses or hypotheses, etc. Until these guesses and hypotheses have been tested, modified and retested, we are still uncomfortable. Even when this is completed, the tension is not relieved until we tell someone what we have discovered or produced. Throughout the process there is an element of responding constructively to existing or new situations, rather than merely adapting to them.

Torrance Tests of Creative Thinking

In 1966, Torrance published the *Torrance Tests of Creative Thinking (TTCT)* which consists of a battery of tasks which measure creative thinking abilities. The *TTCT* is the most widely used and most research creativity test with over 2,000 studies reporting it usage. Although there have been several hundred validity studies of the *TTCT*, perhaps the most powerful evidence of the validity of creativity tests comes from two longitudinal studies: a study of high school student initiated in 1959 and one of elementary school children initiated in 1958. These longitudinal studies with real-life criteria seem to offer the strongest link to test behavior of creative achievement (Torrance, 1988).

Using the *TTCT*, Torrance (1979) has identified a variety of abilities that seem to be important in producing creative responses. Four of the key abilities will be discussed in this chapter. They are:
- fluency - number of responses
- flexibility - number of ways stimuli are used
- originality - unusualness or rarity of the response
- elaboration - number of details that contribute to the response

Fluency

Fluency is the generation of multiple ideas, alternatives or solutions. There is considerable evidence that the more ideas we have, the more likely we are to find a useful solution or answer. Having too few alternatives can be disastrous - merchants with one way of selling tend to fail, parents with one way of disciplining their children have trouble, teachers with one method of teaching fail to meet the learning needs of all students, organizations with one type of program often do not attract sufficient participants and so on.

People have different styles of learning and thinking. We have different motivations and styles of relating to one another. Therefore the creative strength of fluency is of vital importance.

There are many creative techniques for generating ideas, alternatives and solutions. It appears that deliberate training and practice in these methods does produce growth in fluency (Goff, 1992). The need for multiple solutions and options is very apparent in today's world. It is evident that the creative strength of fluency is important and will continue to be of importance in the future.

Brainstorming

One creative technique, which has been used successfully in generating ideas and alternatives, is brainstorming. Brainstorming is the unrestrained offering of ideas or suggestions by all members of a group to seek solutions to problems. Alex Osborn (1963) introduced brainstorming as an element of the creative problem solving method. Brainstorming can be used successfully to stimulate the generation of ideas and facilitate their expression. According to Torrance (1979), brainstorming skills can be developed when practiced with content or when practiced solely for skill development. It is an excellent technique for strengthening fluency, the imagination and communication skills.

Four basic rules govern this process and success depends upon the degree to which we apply them. These rules are:

Rule 1: Criticism is ruled out. Do not criticize or evaluate any idea produced; record any and every idea. This is one of the most important rules and one of the most difficult to master.

Rule 2: Free-wheeling is welcomed. The wilder the idea the better. Off-beat, impractical, silly ideas may trigger a practical, breakthrough idea which might not otherwise occur.

Rule 3: Quantity is desired. The greater the number of ideas produced, the greater the likelihood of useful, original ideas. This includes bringing out those obvious, small ideas as well as the wild, unusual, clever ideas.

Rule 4: Combination and improvement are sought. Combine, hitchhike, improve, change ideas; new ideas lead to more new ideas. Group members are encouraged to hitchhike or think of ways in which the ideas of other members can be turned into better ideas, or how two or more ideas can be combined into a still better idea.

It is extremely important to record every contribution - tape recorder, on the blackboard, flip chart, etc. If the flow if ideas slows down or stops, the facilitator/teacher may ask questions to stimulate the flow (i.e. What if it was much larger or smaller? What if it was a different color or multi-colored? What might other uses be?)

The brainstorming technique gives learners the opportunity to use more brains than one. Generate a multitude of ideas and at least one of them will be truly useful, innovative and workable. Asking learners for their input gives them an added sense of importance and creates and atmosphere for truly creative and imaginative ideas to surface and be acknowledged.

Brainstorming can be used anytime there is a gap in information, a problem, or a question. It is a technique that can be used individually or in groups. Brainstorming provides opportunities to experience active learning and participation. It stimulates and generates enthusiasm as well as promoting spontaneity and creativity. Learners develop an awareness of sensing things from many points of view and experience a supportive environment for their creative expressions.

Brainstorming Practice for Fluency

How many of the following can you identify or brainstorm?

- types of flowers
- things you can't see
- things that smell
- things on a farm
- things in a bathroom
- things that run
- things on a beach
- things you don't do
- names of holidays
- ice cream flavors

- things that are green
- types of animals
- names of colors

Flexibility

Flexibility is the ability to process information or objects in different ways given the same stimulus (Torrance, Wu & Ando, 1980). Flexibility is the ability to abandon old ways of thinking and initiate different directions. It is adaptive when aimed at a solution to a specific problem, challenge or dilemma (Arieti, 1976) and especially important when logical approaches fail to produce satisfactory results (Torrance, 1987).

Optical illusions require flexibility, they require looking from different perspectives in order to see different objects or images. Seeing animals or objects in the clouds requires the flexibility of seeing concrete shapes in cloud formations.

Flexible thinking provides for shifts in thoughts, detours in thinking to include contrasting reasons, differing points of view, alternate plans, differing approaches and various perspectives of a situation (Eberle, 1971). Eberle (1971) developed the SCAMPER technique, a checklist, to assist people in improving their imaginative abilities

SCAMPER TECHNIQUE

S	Substitute	To have a person or thing act or serve in place of another
C	Combine	To bring together, to unite
A	Adapt	To adjust for the purpose of suiting a condition or purpose

M	Modify	To alter, to change the form or quality
	Magnify	To enlarge, to make greater in form or quality
	Minify	To make smaller, lighter, slower, less frequent
P	Put to	To be used for purposes other than originally intended, other uses
E	Eliminate	To remove, omit or get rid of a quality, part or whole
R	Reverse	To place opposite or contrary, to turn it around
	Rearrange	To change order or adjust, different plan, layout or scheme

Another valuable technique for encouraging flexibility is the use of provocative questions. Provocative questions open up a situation to a broader and deeper line of thinking which otherwise might not be produced or considered. They require the learner to think about ideas or concepts they have not thought about previously. Provocative question may be directed at the learner personally with the learner being asked to relate the information to his/her own experiences or future possibilities.

Provocative Questions Requiring Flexibility

1. WHAT COULD HAPPEN IF:
    - every flower in the world was yellow?
    - cats could bark when the wanted to?
    - peas tasted like candy?
2. HOW IS:
    - a spoon like a car?

- a sunset like a dessert?
- a flower like a mountain?
3. WHAT MIGHT HAPPEN IF:
    - it always rained on Saturday?
    - it was against the law to sing?
    - people forgot how to laugh?
4. CAN YOU IMAGINE WHAT MIGHT HAPPEN IF:
    - congress repealed the law of gravity?
    - turkeys were as ferocious as tigers?
    - bicycles could fly?

Originality

Originality involves getting away from the obvious and commonplace or breaking away from habit bound thinking. According to Torrance (1995a), original ideas are statistically infrequent. One possible explanation for this is that an original thinker must be comfortable with being different or a minority of one. The original thinker must be able to withstand the ridicule and skepticism which will be directed toward his/her ideas and himself/herself. One simple way of facilitating originality is to be respectful of unusual ideas or alternatives.

Research has shown that the person who produces a large number of alternatives is more likely to produce original ideas. Brainstorming is one technique which is frequently used to generate ideas and alternatives. Some key elements in increasing the originality of ideas and alternatives produced include:
- providing adequate time to produce alternatives
- choosing problems of importance which arouse emotions

- imaginatively experimenting with various ideas and combinations of ideas
- making it acceptable to produce wild, silly or incredible ideas

Originality is a creative strength which is a mental leap away from the obvious. Original ideas are often described as "unique," "surprising," "wild," "unusual," "unconventional," "novel," "weird," "remarkable," or "revolutionary." According to Torrance (1987), you need courage to be creative. Just as soon as you have a new idea, you are a minority of one. Being a minority of one is uncomfortable - it takes courage. If we can just remember this when we encounter and react to creative ideas and alternatives, we will be more respectful and supportive of originality and original thinkers.

Many art media are conducive to the expression of originality. What appears below is a relaxation scenario involving the use of clay.

Clay Activity for Originality

I. **Warm-up**

Take a deep breath and blow it out. Relax and get comfortable. Again, big breath in . . . hold it . . . exhale . . . . Concentrate on clearing you mind and shutting off your self-talk or internal dialogue. . . . Blow out all of your thoughts with this breath . . . ready, breathe in . . . hold it . . . and exhale . . . You feel relaxed and at ease.

Now I want you to listen closely as I describe this scene. I want you to imagine what I am saying. Some people find it easier to concentrate with their eyes closed. This is optional. (Sometimes, people are

CREATIVE ABILITIES

afraid to close their eyes, so try not to make them feel uncomfortable. I do not know why they are afraid to close their eyes, they must not ever sleep.)

II. Dig-in

Imagine you are walking down a long corridor with narrow walls and soft lights. You hear the sound of music in the distance, music that is vaguely familiar - as if you remember it from many years ago. . . . You reach the end of the corridor and there is a large, round room. . . . Around the room are doors and each door has a number from 1 to 10 on it.

Walk around the room and touch the handle of each door . . . . The number on each door represents that year of your life . . . . You will choose a door that leads to a year that was significant for you . . . a year when you were happy, self-confident and playful.

Feel the handle of the door that you are most drawn to and observe the number on it. . . . Turn the handle and enter the room you have chosen . . . . When you step through that door, be aware that you body feels as it did in that year . . . . The music you heard earlier is playing softly in this room . . . . What is the tune? . . . What else do you hear? . . .What do you see? . . . Toys? . . . Games? . . . What do you smell? . . . Are there smells associated with this time in your life? . . . What about tastes? . . . A favorite candy or treat? . . . How do you feel? . . . Happy? . . . Secure? . . . Playful? . . All of your favorite playthings, your beloved childhood possessions are there . . . . Remember the joy you felt when you spent hours playing and using your imagination . . .

On the count of three, I want you to open your eyes and we'll get to the clay . . Ready, 1 . . .2 . . .3 . . . and you're back. I want you to take the clay you have been provided and recreate the wonderful objects from your childhood.... Show me something special and comforting from you childhood.... Take about 20 minutes to sculpt a good memory or memories from your childhood.

III. Go Beyond

After 20 minutes, ask each member of the group to show and tell about his/her childhood memories. Be sure that everyone has the opportunity to share. Everyone listened to the same scenario and had the same clay, but the products are original, unique to you and your experiences.

After everyone has shared his/her creations, lead a discussion around the following questions.
1. How did this experience make you feel?
2. How difficult was it to imagine childhood memories? Were they in color?
3. How difficult or easy was it to experience your different senses during the scenario reading and while creating the remembered objects/items out of clay?
4. How important is it to be able to use your imaginations and to express your thoughts?
5. What do you think you could learn about people using this activity?

Elaboration

Elaboration is the ability to embellish ideas with details (Torrance, 1979). Elaboration involves implementation and production of a new idea/invention/program. It is essential in producing anything creative that can be recognized, valued and used.

Elaboration involves planning what must be done, who is to do each task, when it is to be done, how it is to be done, how much time it is going to take and how much it is going to cost (Torrance, 1979).

Elaboration involves making the plan, telling the story, filling in the gaps and details, tying up loose ends, orchestrating the activity, coordinating the project, selling the idea/invention, painting a picture with words, etc. Almost always there is resistance to the acceptance of innovation and new ideas of all kinds. It takes a great deal of elaboration of the idea, its implementation, its value and its relationships to others to sell a new idea and gain its acceptance (Torrance, 1979, p. 69).

Practice Activities for Elaboration

1. Design and draw a dog catching machine. First, make up a list of requirements. Then order these requirements according to their importance. Then design the machine.
2. Make up an imaginative story using one of the following titles. Describe the central character of the story as fully as you can and write about one of this character's typical adventures.
   a. The Singing Donkey
   b. The Walking Whale
   c. The Preacher Who Could Not Talk
   d. The Boxer Who Was Afraid
   e. The Two Ton Mouse
   f. The Boy Who Could Fly
   g. The Girl Who Was President of Mars
3. In teams, use recycled materials to create the ideal school of the future in the year 2050. What would it look like? What would a typical school day be

like? Be able to describe and explain your ideal school and school activities.

Summary

All of us have these four creative strengths, but to varying degrees. We utilize different strengths in different settings and that's called "being creative." Dividing creativity into these four principle abilities helps our understanding of the creative strengths of ourselves and others. Experiment with the different techinques discussed in this chapter and see how they work. What are your creative strengths?

For more information on the *TTCT* (Torrance Tests of Creative Thinking) contact Scholastic Testing Service, Inc. at 800-642-6STS for sales or fax: 630-766-8054 or e-mail: STSLH25@aol.com

Chapter 3
LEARNING AND CHILDREN

As children, before we begin our traditional learning experiences, we are expert learners who use all of our senses and motor capabilities to learn. We learn by experiencing, such as sticking a crayon into our mouths, ears, or noses. We learn by seeing what the crayon can do, such as drawing, mashing, eating or crumbling it. We learn by comparing the crayon to other things that mark or are colorful. All of us begin life as experiential learners. It seems logical then to believe that teaching must validate this process of learning by experience in order to meet the needs of all learners, not just those who do well on pre-determined standards.

Learning by doing should not be left to mere chance, but should be part of the guidance we give to learners of all ages. We need to offer opportunities for students to learn core subjects creatively. Creative thinking and learning involve such abilities as evaluation, redefinition, analysis, divergent production and problem solving abilities. Creative learning is a natural, healthy human process that occurs when people become curious or excited about understanding or knowing more. Anytime we are faced with a problem or dilemma with no learned solution, some creativity is required (Torrance, 1995a).

Arousing the curiosity of the learner, providing the learner with sound principles and practices, and making the learning relevant for the student are the three steps in Torrance's educational model of teaching which will be discussed in the next chapter. Learning needs to be fun for both the teacher and learner. Teachers need to foster and nurture the creativity of their students by incorporating assignments that call for original work, independent and interdependent learning, as well as self and group initiated projects involving experimentation, investigation and discovery.

Cooperative learning and group problem solving activities provide valuable opportunities for learners to learn from each other, to learn about each other's differences and strengths, and to gain practical experience by dealing with peers who are culturally, academically or physically not like themselves. Cooperative learning encourages students to demonstrate learning outcomes that are relevant and useful. There is an important difference between putting learners into groups and actually teaching them to care about one another's learning.

Most group experiences I have had in educational settings were not cooperative learning and have not been very beneficial. Usually someone takes charge and tells everyone else what to do, rather than discussing what each person feels comfortable contributing and collectively deciding on the final product or outcome. By calling on groups to do original work or to learn something creatively, there is more of an opportunity for learning and working together. There is more dialogue between group members, because they are all on new ground and are being asked to learn together.

Educational offerings to learners must be practical and useful in more settings than school. Teacher education must provide it's members with practice in new skills being demanded by the public, such as collaboration, flexible thinking and problem solving abilities. Learners must be provided with opportunities to identify strengths and to build upon those strengths by learning the skills of interdependence. If preservice teachers can experience these opportunities, they will be better prepared to facilitate the learning of these skills in their classrooms. Our failure to provide a responsive environment kills much of the excitement of learning at a very early age.

Gender

Our overemphasis or misplaced emphasis on sex roles is a serious block to the development of many talents, especially creative talents (Torrance, 1995a). Creativity, by its very nature, requires both sensitivity and independence. In our culture, sensitivity is a feminine virtue while independence is a masculine virtue. Rarely do women become scientific discoverers, inventors or composers. Very few women have made contributions to theories of creativity.

According to Helson (1978), creative innovation is facilitated by certain social roles that are not usually available to women. Male judges of creative contributions tend to favor work similar to their own. Women's contributions do not customarily receive the same recognition. Pohlman (1996) suggests that creativity may be more of a social process, dramatically affected by social environments and institutions, than simply a psychological trait inherent in individuals.

Creative potential is the ability to respond constructively and in nonhabitual ways to change and stress (Torrance, 1965). Creativity measures are consistently better predictor's of women's adult creative achievements than are measures of intelligence (Torrance, 1972a). IQ tests are based on learning cultivated and valued by men, therefore traditional learning settings may not be the best learning environments for females (Philbin, Meier, Huffman & Boverie, 1995). A substantial body of evidence indicates that males and females perform at similar levels on tests designed to measure creative potential (Torrance, 1983). Landrum (1994) outlines some specific differences between male and female approaches to learning. Through my observations, I would describe the general differences between male and female learners as follows:

> FEMALE APPROACH: negotiation, feelings, understanding, personal relationships, intuitive, other oriented, win-win outcomes

> MALE APPROACH: aggressiveness, competitive, ego-gratifying, impersonal relationships, specific, rule oriented, win-lose outcomes

A growing body of literature on women's development has begun to illuminate issues regarding women's learning styles (Taylor & Marienau, 1995). According to Keohane (1990), a large body of research indicates that girls and boys develop differently and approach learning differently. Studies have shown that women often exhibit similar learning style preferences (Carter, 1990).

In general, women are relational learners. We tend to place emphasis on relevance and personal meaning in what is taught and how we feel about that information. However, most school environments place emphasis on inanimate facts and figures with no opportunities to personalize the learning. The analytical style of most school and work environments generally do not encourage nor foster relational learning thereby denying many girls and women equal opportunities for learning. Kaplan (1995) indicates that new ways of seeing girls and women and human possibilities can come from women bringing their own unique ways of operating to light.

Sensory Learning

All learners begin learning through their senses. Through experiences of touching, smelling, tasting, feeling, hearing and seeing, we learn. Gardner's (1983) theory of multiple intelligences gave fuel to the idea of sensory learning in creating. Gardner proposed seven different kinds of intelligences or learning styles which can be identified and developed. They are:

- Linguistic - the intelligence of words
- Logical-Mathematical - the intelligence of numbers and reasoning
- Spatial - the intelligence of pictures and images
- Musical - the intelligence of tone, rhythm and timbre
- Bodily-Kinesthetic - intelligence of the whole body and movement

- Interpersonal - the intelligence of social understanding
- Intrapersonal - the intelligence of self-knowledge

A method of describing how people process sensory information is called neurolinguistic programming or NLP. The NLP method (Matte & Henderson, 1995) focuses on three sensory processors - visual, auditory and kinesthetic.

According to Matte and Henderson (1995), 55% of our population consists of visual learners. These individuals tend to be fast talkers, gesture freely and communicate clearly and concisely. Individuals who process information visually tend to use visual descriptions when communicating, such as "I see," "Can you picture that?," or "It's clear to me." Visual processors prefer charts, pictures, diagrams and words for optimal learning. A visual learners wants to read it.

Less than 20% of the population consists of auditory learners (Matte & Henderson, 1995). These individuals are sensitive to and easily distracted by sounds. Auditory processors respond positively to presentations with a variety of sounds, tones and rhythms. A monotone voice really turns them off. They use descriptive words involving sound, such as "Can we talk?," "That sounds right," or "It's clear as a bell." Auditory processors prefer lecture, discussions, multimedia presentations and group study to learn best. Auditory learners want to hear it.

About 25% of the population consists of kinesthetic learners (Matte & Henderson, 1995). These individuals are feelings and touch oriented. Kinesthetic processors are good at hands-on tasks, sensitive to the feelings of others and may focus on emotions rather than on logic and reason. They use descriptive words involving touch and emotion, such as "I have a gut feeling", "I sense you're right," or I'm getting a handle on it." Kinesthetic processors prefer hands-on projects, writing down the information and applying it to real life situations to learn best. Kinesthetic learners want to experience it.

Hemisphericity

The human brain consists of two halves - the right hemisphere and the left hemisphere. The right hemisphere controls the left side of the body and the left hemisphere controls the right side of the body. Scientists have learned that each hemisphere has identifiable functions. Knowledge that each half has specific functions was largely derived from observing the effects of brain injuries.

The thick nerve cable with millions of fibers that cross-connects the left and right hemispheres is called the corpus callosum. In the 1950's, Roger Sperry and his students established that the main function of the corpus callosum was to provide communication between the hemispheres and to allow transmission of memory and learning (Edwards, 1979). Their research indicated that the corpus callosum could be severed and two halves would continue to function.

Sperry and his students at California Institute of Technology continued their brain studies, referred to as "split-brain" studies. Based on evidence of the split-brain studies, Sperry (1968) found that both hemispheres use high level thinking skills, though different, both involve thinking, reasoning and complex mental functioning. Scientists have found much support for Sperry's findings not only in brain-injured patients, but also in individuals with intact, healthy brains.

According to pioneering, split-brain surgeon Bogen (1969, p. 157), an individual with two intact hemispheres has the capacity for two distinct minds. Studies of individuals who have undergone "split-brain" operations indicate that the right hemisphere is superior to the left when it comes to coping with the novel and unfamiliar, especially when there are no clues or ways to respond (Restak, 1991). According to Restak (1991), anatomically the right hemisphere is uniquely suited for creativity. The right hemisphere contains many long fibers that connect widely separated regions whereas the left hemisphere contains short fibers that provide richer innerconnections within a region. You might say that the right hemisphere is the generalist, "a jack of all trades" with numerous approaches to problems and the left hemisphere is a specialist with logical, linear approaches to problems. Remember that these two hemispheres or styles of processing information are in each one of us.

Many books have been written on the right and left brains or hemispheres. Research provides evidence of different ways in which the left and right hemispheres of the brain process information (Taggart & Torrance, 1984). Generally, the right hemisphere processes nonverbal information or images and the left hemisphere processes verbal information or words. Edwards (1979, p. 40) provides a good comparison of left and right characteristics:

LEFT		RIGHT	
Verbal:	Uses words to name, describe, define	Non-Verbal	Aware of things, surroundings
Analytic:	Step-by-step, part-by-part	Synthetic:	Puts things together to form whole
Symbolic:	Uses symbols to stand for something	Concrete:	Relates to things as they are, the present moment
Abstract:	Takes small bit of information and uses it to represent the whole	Analogic:	Sees likenesses between things, understands metaphors and analogies
Temporal:	Keeps track of time, uses sequencing - "first things first"	Non-temporal:	Has no sense of time - loses track of time when involved
Rational:	Draws conclusions, wants closure	Non-rational:	Suspends judgment, stays open
Digital:	Uses numbers, follows formulas	Spatial:	Sees things in relation to other things and how parts go to together to make a whole
Logical:	Draws conclusions based on logic, uses reason and a logical order	Intuitive:	Makes leaps of insight, goes by hunches, feelings and visions

Most traditional education provides encouragement and instruction for the left hemispheric style of learning whereas the right hemispheric style of learning is generally left to develop by chance and is often actively discouraged.

Cooperative Learning

Demographic trends suggest that by the year 2000, 33% of our nation will be members of ethnic and minority groups (Putnam, 1993). Schools are being asked to assume ever-expanding roles, to address societal problems ranging from violence to drug abuse, poverty, discrimination and segregation (Phipho, 1992). The goal of education is shifting from preparing students to enter an economy based on manufacturing to the preparation of individuals who can function in a highly technological, service-oriented, mobile society.

One of the pressing duties of educators is responding to the needs of academically as well as culturally diverse students within the classroom. An inclusive classroom is one in which the members recognize each other's differences and strive to support one another's efforts. Cooperative learning environments benefit from diversity. It is diversity or the differences (strengths, talents, skills, ideas) that make cooperative learning so powerful.

More than 800 studies had been conducted on cooperative learning by 1989 (Johnson & Johnson). These studies indicate that cooperative learning situations result in higher student self-esteem and improved peer relations. Cooperative learning, versus segregated and competitive learning, increases the academic achievement and social acceptance of learners regardless of culture or abilities.

According to Resnick (1990), learning is a social act, more closely related to the process of socialization than to simply instruction. Cooperative learning engages learners in the observation of and participation in socially and culturally acceptable models for learning. Authentic cooperative learning activities encourage individuals to demonstrate learning outcomes that have relevance and enable a learner to succeed in current and future environments (Glasser, 1986).

Cooperative learning requires communication among group members while they work on assigned tasks. Learners are expected to interact with one another as they take on roles, collectively engage in solving problems, explain their thinking to one another and discuss ways to resolve conflicts as they arise. Common understandings are arrived at only when the individuals in the group are able to present their points of view and to discuss their perspectives on problems (Williams, 1993). The necessary features of successful cooperative learning experiences are: positive interdependence, individual accountability, interaction, communication and discussion.

In cooperative learning activities, individuals learn:
- to deal with differences
- to recognize each other's strengths
- to show respect by acknowledging the contributions of all group members to the task at hand
- to take turns
- to gain practical experience in dealing with peers who are culturally, academically or physically not like themselves

- to engage in the process of sharing their experiences and ideas

Some of the positive outcomes from a cooperative learning environments include:
1. increased achievement levels of all learners
2. individuals tend to feel better about themselves when given opportunities for success and self-expression
3. learners accept differences more readily in and out of the learning environment

Cooperative learning environments are important in more settings than just schools. With more and more women entering the work force, more attention will be paid to cooperative learning experiences since cooperative learning is generally a preferred learning style of women.

Creativity and Children

Young children are experts in creative ways of learning. They have considerable experience learning through all of their senses as they manipulate, investigate, explore, experiment and play in an effort to understand and find truth. When there is something that a young child does not understand they do something about it by making guesses, asking questions, testing, revising and retesting. When they discover something or learn how something works, they want to tell someone about it. This is a natural, creative process. At times it is lightning quick, automatic and spontaneous. At other times, there must be time for one thing to lead to another.

Young children are full of the spirit of wonder and imagination. They tend to prefer to learn in creative ways, trying to discover how things work or why things are the way they are. When children are learning in creative ways, they become completely absorbed and have long attention spans.

Creative young children may insist on learning in creative ways rather than by authority in predetermined ways (Torrance, 1975a). Young creative children use their imaginations to solve problems. They are terrific storytellers and can compose stories, songs and poems in enchanting and exciting ways.

Society has been very harsh in its treatment of creative children, who will almost inescapably come into conflict with authorities in the system. All children, especially creative children, must have the right to "fail" (learn what doesn't work) without being ridiculed and ostracized (Torrance, 1972a). Creative young children need encouragement and support in finding legitimate and appropriate ways of expressing themselves and communicating their ideas. Children who have little chance to use their creative abilities in socially acceptable ways are very likely to express themselves in illegal and destructive ways. Education needs to be much more responsive to different learning styles in order to truly meet the needs of all children!

Fantasy, for example, is one of the favorite ways of learning among young children. Their imaginations need to be kept alive, developed and guided. Many adults try hard to eliminate fantasy by the time a child enters school. They do this because they believe fantasy is unhealthy. However, imaginative role playing, telling fantastic stories, making unusual drawings and paintings are normal aspects of children's thinking and problem solving.

Young children are naturally curious. They wonder about people and their world. By the time they enter preschool, they already have a variety of learning skills acquired through questioning, inquiring, searching, manipulating, experimenting, and playing. They are content to watch from a distance at first, however, this does not satisfy their curiosity. Children need opportunities for a closer look; they need to touch; they need time for the creative encounter.

We place many restrictions on children's desire to explore their world. We discourage them by saying "Curiosity killed the cat." If we were honest, we would admit that curiosity makes a good cat and that cats are extremely skilled in testing the limits and determining what is safe and what is dangerous. Apparently children, as well as cats, have an irresistible tendency to explore objects and this very tendency seems to be the basis for the curiosity and inventiveness of adults. Even in testing situations, children who do the most manipulating of objects, produce the most ideas and the largest number of original ideas (Torrance & Goff, 1990).

How Adult's "Kill" Creativity

Many times adults do not even realize that they have an effect on the creative development of children. Children understand actions more than they understand the words we use to describe those actions. For example, when we tell a child to be quiet when he/she is asking a question leads him/her to believe that asking questions is not a good thing. Here

are a several ways in which adults kill the creativity of children:
- Insisting that children do things the "right way" all of the time. Teaching a child to think that there is just one right way to do things kills the urge to try new ways.
- Pressuring children to be realistic, to stop imagining and fantasizing. When we label the child's flights of fantasy as "silly," we bring the child down to earth with a thud, causing the inventive urge to curl up and die.
- Making comparisons with other children. This is a subtle pressure on a child to conform; yet the essence of creativity is freedom to choose whether to conform or not to conform.
- Discouraging children's curiosity. One of the surest indicators of creativity is curiosity; yet we often brush questions aside because we are too busy for "silly" questions. Children's questions deserve respect.

Maybe as adults we are secretly jealous of children's playfulness and innocence. We then act in ways that undermine the curiosity and creative expression of children in order to get them to be more like adults. But really, being an adult isn't much fun if you can't be childlike, so we need to retrain our thinking to celebrate and join in the excitement of learning and creating. Only when we have a balance of play and work in our lives are we truly peaceful and happy.

What Can Teachers Do?

Wise teachers can offer a curriculum with plenty of opportunities for creative behaviors. They can make assignments that call for original work, independent learning, self-initiated projects, cooperative learning experiences and experimentation. Using curriculum materials that provide progressive warm-up experiences, procedures that permit one thing to lead to another rather than along a prescribed path, and activities that make creative thinking both legitimate and rewarding make it easier for teachers to provide opportunities for creative learning.

The following are some things caring teachers can do to foster and nurture the creativity of children:

- We can teach children to appreciate and be pleased with their own creative efforts.
- We can be respectful of the unusual and hard to answer questions children ask.
- We can be respectful of children's unusual ideas and solutions, for all children will see many relationships that their parents and teachers miss.
- We can show children that their ideas have value by listening to their ideas and considering them. We can encourage children to test their ideas by using them and communicating them to others. We must give them credit or recognition for their ideas.
- We can provide opportunities and give credit for self-initiated learning. Overly detailed supervision, too much reliance on predetermined curricula, failure to appraise learning resulting from a child's own initiative, and attempts to cover too much

material with no opportunity for reflection interfere seriously with creative learning.
- We can provide chances for children to learn, think and discover without threats of immediate evaluation. Constant evaluation, especially during practice and initial learning, makes children afraid to use creative ways to learn. We must accept their honest errors as part of the creative process and their problem solving efforts.
- We can establish creative relationships with children by encouraging creativity in the classroom while providing adequate guidance and support for learning.

What Can Parents/Grandparents/Guardians do?

It is natural for young children to learn creatively by dancing, singing, storytelling, playing make believe, and so forth. One of the first challenges to creativity may be formal schooling. By this time, parents, grandparents as well as teachers, appreciate conforming behaviors such as being courteous and obedient, following rules, and being like others. While these are desirable traits to some extent, they may also destroy a child's creative potential.

The following are some positive ways parents/grandparents/guardians can foster and nurture the growth of creativity:
- Encourage curiosity, exploration, experimentation, fantasy, questioning, testing and the development of creative talents.
- Provide opportunities for creative expression, creative problem solving, and constructive response to change and stress.

- Prepare children for new experiences and help develop creative ways of coping with them.
- Find ways of changing destructive behavior into constructive, productive behavior rather than relying on punitive methods of control (punishment).
- Make sure that every member of the family receives individual attention, respect and is given opportunities to make significant, creative contributions to the welfare of the family as a whole.
- Use what the school provides imaginatively and supplement the school's efforts.
- Give the child purpose, commitment and courage.

For more activities and a play dough recipe, see APPENDIX A.

Summary

We have so much to learn about supporting the growth and development of all learners. Much of what is discussed in this chapter revolves around respect. If we teach our children to respect each other and each other's strengths, we will be well on our way to making this world a better place for all of us. Our future generations will be required to solve the problems we are creating today. They'll have to be darned good problem solvers too.

Chapter 4
CREATIVE LEARNING AND INCUBATION

Incubation involves the flashes of insight while in the process of puzzling over a problem or dilemma, mulling it over, fitting the pieces together, trying to figure it out. Incubation is the part of the creative learning process that calls for little or no conscious effort. It is the time between being engulfed in a problem or saturated with information pertaining to the problem you are solving and the flash of insight with a solution. The flashes of insight come while you are going to sleep, taking a shower, reading a newspaper, sitting outside, relaxing or playing.

In the incubation stage, we step back from the problem and let our minds contemplate and work it through. Incubation involves contemplation, subconscious processing, reflection, mulling, visualization and sensory perception (Hermann, 1987). According to Osborn (1963, p. 314), the part of the creative process that calls for little or no conscious effort is known as incubation. To incubate means "to lie down" which carries a connotation of purposive relaxation. In its application to the workings of imagination, the term covers the phenomenon by which ideas spontaneously well up into our conscious mind.

Torrance and Safter (1990) give the example of asking graduate students to incubate about something, some students had insights before coming to class - in the shower, while shaving, while eating breakfast or upon awakening. However, if they were asked to articulate their insights, most of the others began having their flashes "right then." They could not have had these, however, unless they had been incubating (Torrance & Safter, 1990, p. 30).

The incubation process is a critical element in creative learning. Unless time is allowed for one thing to lead to another, there is little possibility of finding a really creative solution. Supportive, nurturing environments allow time for learners to think, to mull ideas over and incubate.

Supportive Learning Environments

Creating an environment that facilitates creative thinking and encourages time for incubation will facilitate the development of important creative processes and the overall development of creativity. The first hurdle is creating an atmosphere where learners have confidence expressing themselves and sharing their thoughts and ideas. This requires the leader/teacher to defer judgment, to allow time for one thing to lead to another, to encourage discussion and questions, to respect each and every thought or idea expressed, and to allow the learner to find his/her own acceptable solution.

If learners are not familiar with this type of nurturing environment, they may try to take advantage of the situation or rebel. It requires patience and persistence on the part of the teacher to allow the learner the freedom to explore while at the same time staying focused on the learning situation at hand. The teacher must allow the learner time to incubate and think during the learning process. Usually, the learners test the situation in order to determine if the leader/teacher can be trusted and if they will be truly respected.

At first, the learners are hesitant to engage in active, participatory learning. It may take several weeks or months to get the learners comfortable with the idea that they share in the responsibility for learning. Also, it tests the constitution of a teacher to allow the learners to determine their own answers and solutions or to test and examine the current truths. Once the learner connects with his/her intrinsic motivation for learning, little external motivation and less time, on the part of the teacher, is required.

Providing an environment that supports creative thinking will call upon the creativity of the teacher. Consistency, patience, persistence and an abundance of ideas and time are critical ingredients for nurturing and maintaining the creativity of learners.

Incubation Model of Teaching

Torrance spent 22 years developing a three-stage instructional model for facilitating the creative learning process (Torrance & Safter, 1990). The three stages of Torrance's Incubation Model of Teaching are: 1) warm-up, 2) dig-in, 3) go beyond. The purpose of the warm-up stage is to heighten anticipation and expectation, to motivate the learners to try to see connections between what they are being asked to learn and something meaningful in their lives. The warm-up stage arouses curiosity, stimulates participation and creates the desire for more information.

Warm-up is necessary, but not enough. We must go beyond the surface, dig in, defer judgment and keep open to new information and insights. The second stage or dig-in stage, involves encountering the expected and unexpected, deepening expectations and assimilating the new information. There must be time for one thing to lead to another.

In order for new information to become part of our thinking and actions, we must apply it to real life and give it personal meaning. During the third stage, personal experiences are related to the information, the information is given personal meaning and then applied in real world situations. The third stage requires incubation and time for one thing to lead to another.

Torrance's Incubation Model of Teaching (Torrance & Safter, 1990, p. 8):

I. **Warm-up**
- create the desire to know
- get attention
- heighten anticipation and expectation
- arouse curiosity
- tickle the imagination
- give purpose and motivation

II. **Dig-in**
- digging deeper
- looking twice
- listening for smells
- crossing out mistakes
- cutting holes to see through
- getting in deep water

CREATIVE LEARNING AND INCUBATION

- getting out of locked doors

III. Go Beyond
- having a ball
- singing in one's own key
- building sand castles
- plugging into the sun
- shaking hands with tomorrow

Summary

It's as easy as 1-2-3. First, get someone interested in the topic. People often use ice breakers for warm-ups. Warm-up is where you get the audience to participate and be a part of the learning experience. Second, is learning the meat of the topic and gaining competency with the information or skills. Third, relating what is learned to real life which requires being creative.

I have used the Incubation Model to teach all kinds of classes to people of all ages. Once people get used to the idea that they are partners in the learning experience, they become self-motivated to learn. It is a very powerful learning tool that gives structure to a learning activity while allowing time for incubation and encouraging creativity.

It takes courage to be creative since creativity involves taking risks and venturing into the unknown. That is why a supportive, nurturing learning environment is necessary for creativity to occur. We are more likely to try something new if we think we won't be embarrassed or ridiculed. Encouragement is such a wonderful thing!

Everyday Creativity: An Easty-to-Read Guide

Strengths
- Common sense
- gentle hearted
- humor
- Collaboration
- Persistent

"What else?"

Chapter 5
CREATIVITY AND PERSONAL STRENGTHS

Traditional tests have neglected the competencies important to real-world performance. It is important to understand the motives that drive us and satisfy us in real world settings. Existing research on adults' everyday cognition, in general, has not yet shown that traditional measures of intelligence are good predictors of real world outcomes (e.g., self-confidence, persistence, physical and emotional well-being, life satisfaction, courage).

The intelligence testing movement originated in attempts to predict academic competence, and so concerned itself with the prediction of school performance (Marsiske & Willis, in press). Using familiar situations with prior knowledge and reasoning may be sufficient to solve some problems or dilemmas. However, there are instances in everyday life in which new and different problems and dilemmas emerge, which require some cognitive bridging or creativity.

Since creativity is a term ordinarily reserved for exceptional individuals and extraordinary accomplishments, recognizing it in the practical, problem solving activities of ordinary people introduces a new perspective for investigation (Scribner, 1986). Research on the adult development of creativity related mental abilities has not been nearly as extensive as research conducted on intellectual abilities.

American psychology has busily occupied itself with only half of the picture of life and has neglected the other and perhaps more important half (Maslow, 1987). Maslow (1987) declared that science must account for all reality, not just the tidy, sequential portions of it. In 1971, Maslow mischievously said that science could be defined as a technique whereby noncreative people can create (p. 60).

However, there have been some creative people researching the positives of life. A more positive psychology, the other side, has developed and is based on theories of growth. Growth theories emphasize the realization of a person's full potential.

Maslow distinguished between "special talent creativeness" and "self-actualizing creativeness." Most creativity research has been conducted on "special talent creativeness." Very little research has been conducted on "self-actualizing creativeness." This chapter will focus on the "self-actualizing creativeness" of everyday people.

Creativity and Self-Actualization

Abraham Maslow was a pioneer, philosopher and foremost spokesman for humanistic psycholgies. He questioned and explored human psychology creating a positive and whole view of human nature. He discovered that human functioning was different for people who operate in a state of positive health rather than a state of deficiency. Maslow was one of the most influential psycholgists and important contributors to our modern view of human nature.

Maslow (1959) developed the concept of self-actualization and defined it as an ongoing process of making growth choices. According to Maslow (1971), self-actualization means experiencing fully, vividly, selflessly, with full concentration and total absorption (p. 45). Maslow (1971) theorized that the concept of creativeness and the concept of the healthy, self-actualizing, fully human person may be one and the same.

Self-actualization may be described as the full use and exploitation of talents, capacities, potentialities and the like. Such people seem to be fulfilling themselves and doing the best that they are capable of doing. They are people who have developed or are developing to the full stature of which they are capable (Maslow, 1987).

Maslow studied the creativity of people who were positively healthy, highly evolved and mature, i.e. self-actualizing. He identified the following characteristics of self-actualizing creativeness (Maslow, 1987, p. 160-164):

- perception - fresh appreciation and wonder of the basic good of life; live more in the real world of nature than the verbalized world of concepts, expectations and beliefs
- expression - ability to express ideas and impulses spontaneously and without fear of ridicule from others
- childlike - innocence of perception and expressiveness, natural, spontaneous, simple, true, pure, uncritical
- affinity for the unknown - open to experience; positively attracted by the unknown, the mysterious, the puzzling

- resolution of dichotomies - ability to synthesize, unify, integrate; able to put separate and even opposite together into unity
- peak experiences - fearless, wonderful, ecstatic experiences which change the person and his/her perception of life

Maslow found that creativity is a universal characteristic of self-actualizing people. They are more spontaneous, more natural, more human than average. The creativeness of self-actualizing people seems to be kin to the naive and universal creativeness of unspoiled children (Maslow, 1987). According to Maslow (1987), all self-actualizing people are always creative. Self-actualizing creativeness stresses the qualities of (Maslow, 1987, p. 167):
- boldness
- courage
- freedom
- spontaneity
- integration
- self-acceptance

Self-actualizing people are very strong people with strong ethical and moral standards. Self-actualizing people infrequently allow convention to hamper them or inhibit them from doing anything they consider very important or basic. Their codes of ethics tend to be relatively autonomous and individual rather than conventional. Their ethics are not necessarily the same as those of the people around them.

Self-actualizing people look out upon the world with wide, uncritical, undemanding, innocent eyes, simply noting and observing what is the case, without either arguing the matter or demanding that it be otherwise. Self-actualizing creativeness is "emitted," like radioactivity, and it hits all of life, regardless of the problems. It is emitted like sunshine; it spreads all over the place; it makes some things grow and is wasted on rocks and other ungrowable things (Maslow, 1987, p. 167).

Personal Strengths

Our ability to deal with the daily dilemmas and problems which we have never faced or dealt with before is based on our creative abilities and strengths. Most of us are keenly aware of our weaknesses and rarely aware of our strengths. When asked to identify personal strengths, most people have great difficulty. Since most of the traditional emphasis in psychology has been on weaknesses, it is not surprising that we know so little about our strengths - what we do well.

In life there are doers and knockers. The doers aren't afraid of failing and are busy trying to accomplish. They are building houses for Habitat for Humanity, or working for the Humane Society or donating to the Red Cross. The knockers are the critics of the world. They sit back and judge everything - nothing is spared and nothing is ever quite good enough. They complain about the homeless, but do nothing to help them. They gripe about stray and neglected animals, but do nothing about the problem. Knockers are full of opinions, not actions. The real doers never knock and the nondoers use knocking as an excuse for not doing. Being a critic takes time and energy and is a passive way of kidding ourselves into thinking we're doing.

There are several reasons why a person is a doer or a knocker. Self-criticism is the worst reason. It paralyzes us from experiencing life. One of the most draining of all self-criticisms is regret. To regret having done or not done something is self-defeating. We did what we had to do at the time and did the best we could at the time. We now know that we can do it better the next time. According to Henry Ford, failure is only the opportunity to more intelligently begin again. There is no disgrace in honest failure; there is disgrace in fearing to fail.

If we could objectively look at our lives, we would see that most of the events which happened were not caused by us at all. Most situations and events that occur in our lives do so without us lifting a finger and without us having any "control" at all. It happened because it was meant to happen.

Free will and choice are attributes of the mind that most of us tend to forget. We are generally so focused on self-criticism and worry that we forget to use our imaginations. We have all had the experience of feeling trapped in a situation and unable to escape. By using our active imaginations, we can find a way out. Problems are opportunities for learning. We can experience a sense of joy and well-being when the lessons are learned.

Another very draining self-criticism is guilt. Guilt is a form of manipulation usually given to us by another. Again, we punish ourselves for having done something wrong. "Should" is the stick we use to beat ourselves. "Should" never has been and never will be. When we stop comparing what is right here and now with what we wish were true, we can begin to enjoy what is.

We aren't what we think we are, but what we *think*, we are! (Anthony, 1984). We can't help the way we feel about things, but we can help the way we think about them and how we react to them. Punishing ourselves for what did or did not happen is wasted energy. What happened, happened, so get on with life.

Fear of Failure

Fear of failure, fear of criticism, fear of letting someone down or just fear of trying something new, stops many of us from achieving our potential. Most fears are worry and anxiety and consist of false events that appear to be real. Even though many people long for something better, the need for approval and the comfort of the familiar are usually far stronger than the desire to do what they really want.

Knockers believe that the energy they put into maintaining the status quo is actually resisting change. Knockers actually begin to believe that they are holding things together and are in control. However, control is an illusion. Most of life is out of our control and only when we learn to accept things that come into our lives, will we be free from the pain of resistance and able to accept change. In acceptance of change there is peace, in resistance to change there is pain. We must remember that change is always an option.

Most of us go through life with the belief system that our happiness or unhappiness is largely determined by the events in our environment and reactions of others to us. We forget that peace of mind is an internal matter and that it is from a peaceful mind that a peaceful world is experienced. The temptations to react with anger, depression or excitement, exists because of our interpretations and perceptions of the outside world. We can change our interpretations and perceptions anytime, anyway or anywhere.

Inner peace can only be reached when we practice forgiveness. It is through forgiveness that we change our perceptions and let go of our fears, condemning, judgments and grievances. Forgiveness is a process of letting go and overlooking whatever we thought was done to us or what we think we have done to others.

Many of us have learned to believe we can "improve" ourselves by a very cruel system of self-regulation and abuse. We tend to be hard on ourselves and would never consider being that hard on anyone else. We must learn that being kind to ourselves lets us be kinder to others. We can only be compassionate and understanding of others to the degree that we are compassionate and understanding of ourselves.

Whether life is seen as an opportunity (doer) or a burden (knocker) depends on our perspective or point of view, not our circumstances. We can keep looking for the things we don't like in life and knock it or we can look for the things we do like in life and enjoy it. It's a choice.

Parental Strengths

While working in the field of developmental disabilities, I incorporated my interest in creative strengths with my job. Part of my job was delivering community trainings in creativity, communication and collaboration skills. At every training, I asked adult participants to identify and write the strength(s) s/he brought to a collaborative process. They were provided with colored markers and a self-adhesive label to illustrate or write their strengths. This activity was usually greeted with silence and concerned looks.

After everyone had a chance to label themselves according to their strengths, we went around the room and documented the strength(s) of each participant on a paper flip chart. We discussed how much more difficult it was it identify what we are good at than it would have been to identify what we do not do well.

By putting these strengths "up on the board" each participant was acknowledged and included. Each group member was identified by what s/he did well and would probably most like to contribute. Once we had a list of strengths of the participants we could examine the list to determine what strengths were missing. Then each group could decide how to deal with the missing strengths and how to organize around their strengths.

It is from these lists of strengths that a parental strength survey was created. A pilot group of 187 parents of children/youth/adults with disabilities was sent the survey. Seventy-six (41%) of those parents responded in a two week period. To date, eight-six surveys have been collected.

Survey participants were asked to identify which strengths they possess from a checklist of 40 indicators. These indicators were a blend of individual creative abilities and personal strengths identified during courses and trainings. Seventy-six of the respondents were female and ten were male. They varied in ages from 20 to 80 years of age. The majority of the respondents were Caucasian, in good to excellent health and with a median income of $40-50,000. The frequency distributions and percentages of the top ten responses are presented in Table 1.

The most commonly identified strength was that they were responsible individuals. The majority of the parents felt they were empathetic, gentle hearted and considerate of the feelings of others. They felt they had good common sense, a good sense of humor and were good listeners. Being able to see different perspectives/approaches to common problems and being able to improvise with what is available demonstrates flexible thinking. Being persistent and resourcefulness are crucial elements of creativity. Parents and guardians must be creative to deal with day-to-day surprises and occurrences. Much more work needs to

TABLE 1
What's Right with Families:
Parental Strengths Survey

Frequency Distributions and Percentages		
Variable/Strength	Freq.	Percent
1. responsible	80	93
2. empathetic and gentle hearted	75	87
3. have good common sense	74	86
4. good sense of humor	73	85
5. good at considering the feelings of others	72	84
6. good listener	71	83
7. see different perspectives/approaches to common problems	67	78
8. able to improvise with what is available	66	77
9. persistent	65	76
10. creative and resourceful	65	76
Note: N = 86		

be done to better understand what we do well, or strengths. These ten personal strengths of parents who are required to be creative everyday just to survive give us a good beginning. This is a wonderful example of a mother being creative to address an everyday problem (Fobes, 1993, p. 9):

> A mother had a son who threw temper tantrums: lying on the floor, pounding his fists, kicking his legs, and whining for whatever he wanted. One day while in a supermarket he threw one of his temper tantrums. In a moment of desperation, the mother dropped to the floor, pounded her fists, kicked her feet, and whined, "I wish you'd stop throwing temper tantrums!"
>
> By this time, the son had stood up. He said in a hushed tone, "Mom, there are people watching? You're embarrassing me!" The mother calmly stood up, brushed off the dust, and said in a clear, calm voice, "That's what you look like when you're throwing a temper tantrum." Sometimes, traditional approaches such as bribery, threatening, ignoring or giving in seem so natural that we overlook the possibility that something different, such as embarrassment, might work too.

Collaborations

Effective collaborations involve the use of the strengths of the individual members in a problem solving process. It is a purposeful relationship formed to solve a problem, create or discover something or to change something. Successful collaborations require a balance of the four creative abilities of fluency, flexibility, originality and elaboration. It is from these creative strengths that people can truly contribute.

Collaborations are formed when we realize that we cannot do it all by ourselves. We need insights, comments, questions and ideas from others. Other perspectives add value and richness to our own. In effective collaborations, people learn to identify their strengths and talents as well as increase self-esteem by sharing and achieving common goals. According to deBono, achievement is one of life's more durable joys.

The anonymous goose story captures the essence of collaboration:

Goose Story

When you see geese flying along in a V formation . . .you might consider what science has discovered as to why they fly that way. As each bird flaps its wings, it creates an uplift for the bird immediately following. By flying in a V formation the whole flock adds at least 71% greater flying range than if each bird flew on its own. People who share a common direction and sense of community can get where they are going more quickly and easily because they are traveling on the thrust of one another.

When a goose falls out of formation it suddenly feels the drag and resistance of trying to go it alone and quickly gets back into formation to take advantage of the lifting power of the bird in front. If we have as much sense as a goose we will stay in formation with those who are headed in the same direction we are.

When the head goose gets tired it rotates back in the formation and another goose flies point. It is sensible to take turns doing demanding jobs . . .with people or with geese flying south.

Geese honk from behind to encourage those up front to keep up their speed. What do we say when we honk from behind?

Finally . . . and it is important . . . when a goose sets sick or is wounded by gunshots, and falls out of formation, two other geese fall out with that goose and follow it down to lend help and protection. They stay with the fallen goose until it is able to fly or until it dies; and only then do they launch out on their own, or with another formation, to catch up with their group. If we have the sense of a goose we will stand by each other like that.

Summary

In a healthy, supportive environment there is virtually no destructive behavior. A good society is one in which good human relations are fostered and encouraged. A good society is a psychologically healthy society. The good society is one that has its institutional arrangements set up in such a way as to foster, encourage, reward and produce a maximum of good human relationships and a minimum of bad human relationships (Maslow, 1987).

From his studies of healthy people, Maslow (1971) became interested in developing a new kind of education which fostered the process person, the creative person, the improvising person and the self-trusting, courageous person. This education would teach an appreciation of beauty and nature. It would focus on the wonders of life and it would teach that life is precious. This education would create healthy, supportive environments for learning through growth.

We are so much more than science has discovered. As we approach more global relationships, we will need to discuss strengths in terms of helping each other instead of conquering each other. Our focus on strengths must be from the position of mutual gain instead of winning and losing. It is from our strengths, as individuals, as communities, as states, as nations, that we will grow and prosper.

Chapter 6
CREATIVE PROBLEM SOLVING

Survival often depends on our ability to make personal adjustments. Making personal adjustments means changing a behavior in order to successfully adapt to a new or different situation. Personal adjustments require an individual to adapt and cope with new experiences and changing situations which occur throughout life. Our ability to make personal adjustments necessary throughout life depends on our creative problem solving skills.

Creative problem solving skills operate at the most general level and can influence performance in any domain (Amabile, 1989). These skills can be influenced by training and by experience. Torrance (1957) found that elements of a creative solution can be taught, but the creativity itself must be self-discovered and self-disciplined.

There is a big difference between getting ideas and doing something about them. An idea all by itself is nice, but doesn't mean much unless it's attached to people and things. The value of ideas comes when you apply them. It's the results the idea bring that makes them valuable. Creative problem solving takes a "proactive" stance of looking for ways to solve the problem, choosing the most promising and acting on it.

Most of us have not had much practice in creative problem solving techniques. Most of the problem solving techniques we practiced while in school involved problems that:
1) have been solved many times
2) the problem is obvious, labeled and numbered
3) have a clearly stated goal
4) have all of the information needed
5) have rules to follow
6) usually have one right answer
7) have someone to evaluate the answer
8) the motivation is for external approval - a grade, reward, approval...

The traditional problem solving method, which is good in a laboratory, is not very applicable to the unknown, ever changing problems of real life. Creative problem solving is what we use to survive every day of our lives, yet we get very little practice using these skills in our structured, supervised, learning environments. In creative problem solving:
1) the problem has not been solved before
2) defining the problem is the hardest part
3) the goal must be identified and clarified
4) the available information is scarce, incorrect, missing, irrelevant, etc.
5) the rules must be determined
6) there are many solutions, none of which is obviously better than another
7) as far as you know, no one knows whether your answer is good or not
8) the motivation is to relieve personal discomfort

Creative Problem Solving Model

In the 1950's Alex Osborn wrote extensively about the importance of imagination and creativity in solving problems. In *Applied Imagination*, Osborn (1953) described many basic steps to help groups and individuals be more successful in creative thinking. Parnes (1967) recognized the power of Osborn's ideas and extended his basic concepts into a systematic approach to creative problem solving.

Parnes (1992) created a five step creative problem solving model for approaching problems in an imaginative way. Throughout all five steps, a problem solver defers judgment during the generation of ideas and alternatives to avoid inhibiting the wildest possibilities which stretch us to better ideas. A problem solver frees him/herself from the natural tendency to judge an idea as good or bad before saying it, writing it or even thinking about it. There are five steps in the Parnes creative problem solving model (Parnes, 1997). They are:

STEP 1- FACT FINDING
Observe carefully and objectively, like a camera, while collecting information about the problem situation. Explore and identify the facts of the situation
ACTION: Who?, What?, Where?, When?, Why?, How (is and is not)?

STEP 2 - PROBLEM FINDING
Clarify the challenge or problem by considering different ways of viewing and speculate on those possibilities.
ACTION: In what ways might we . . .? How do we. . .?

STEP 3 - IDEA FINDING
Seek more diverse ideas, alternatives, options, paths, ways, approaches, various methods and techniques. Find potential solutions from brainstormed ideas.
ACTION: Make new relationships, associations, connections, magnify, minify, combine, rearrange, change, reverse, turn upside down and inside out

STEP 4 - SOLUTION FINDING
Examine ideas in new and different ways, from even more viewpoints and criteria; become aware of consequences, implications, reactions to tentative idea/solution. Select or combine ideas to create a plan of action.
ACTION: Effect on whom? Effect on what? How to improve?

STEP 5 - ACCEPTANCE FINDING
Develop a plan of action, considering all audiences that must accept the plan. Seek ways of making the idea/solution more workable, acceptable, stronger, more effective, more beneficial.
ACTION: What objections will different groups have with the idea/plan? How might we set this plan into action? Who is going to do what?

Much of the considerable research into creative problem solving (Maier, 1970; Torrance, 1979) indicates that a willingness to consider alternatives, to take some risks, to venture into uncertain territory, and to tolerate some ambiguity are important ingredients of effective thinking (Isaksen & Treffinger, 1985).

CREATIVE PROBLEM SOLVING

Dr. Torrance and his wife Pansy began the Future Problem Solving Program using Parnes' five step creative problem solving model to teach youth an interdisciplinary approach to studying and solving future problems. The Future Problem Solving Program was introduced in 1974-75 to 23 high schools in Northeast Georgia. Today the program has grown to over 500,000 participants in dozens of countries. A community problem solving component has been added and adults are included in learning how to take steps today to creatively solve the problems of the future.

Recycling

Recycling has come to the awareness of many people and communities. It is a creative solution to an ever increasing problem - waste disposal. The population of this country represents only 5% of the world's population and produces over 50% of its waste. Americans have traditionally been conditioned to think of things that are old, empty, worn or broken as useless, so they are cast aside and thrown away without much thought. We continue to be wasteful because we cannot think of anything better to do with last year's catalogs, a bunch of empty bottles or a coat with holes in the sleeves. We are just beginning to exploit the resources in our trash.

Many times we cannot think of what on earth to do with our discards. One rule of thumb is if you can't use them yourself, you can't sell them, you don't have a way to recycle them, then try giving them away. Often times we want to get rid of an object before it is worn out. This item could be used if it was just matched with someone who wanted it or could use it. That is the idea behind the Swap Box.

A Swap Box is literally a cardboard box that can be decorated to sit in a room to hold usable, recyclable objects and materials. Learners are asked to bring reusable objects to put into the Swap Box. These items may be magazines, toys, empty containers, records, scraps of material, etc. Anyone who wants something in the box takes it and leaves a discard of his/her own. Before long, there will be a lively exchange going on with people finding things they want and getting rid of things they don't want. Check the Swap Box periodically and remove things have gone unclaimed for a couple of weeks. The following list of craft recyclables can be shared with students in order to get the Swap Box started.

Craft Recyclables

Aerosol-can tops	Aluminum containers	Beads
Beans	Bottle caps and tops	Boxes
Brushes	Buttons	Burlap
Calendars	Candle stubs	Cardboard
Carpet scraps	Chalk	Christmas cards
Cloth scraps	Clothespins	Coat hangers
Coffee cans	Cookie cutters	Corks
Cotton	Crayon stubs	Egg cartons
Fabric	Feathers	Felt
Fur	Fruit cartons	Gift wrap
Gloves	Ice cream containers	Jar lids
Lace	Leather	Linoleum scraps
Magazines	Meat trays (cleaned)	
Mirrors	Milk cartons (cleaned)	Oatmeal boxes
Paper bags	Paper of all kinds	
Paper towel rolls	Pie tins	Plastic bags
Plastic containers	Ribbon rolls	Rope and string
Rug samples	Seeds	Sewing trim
Shells	Socks	Spools
Straws	Toilet paper rolls	Wallpaper scraps
Wood scraps	Yarn	

CREATIVE PROBLEM SOLVING

Recycling Common Place Materials

CANS - were invented in 1810 by an Englishman named Peter Durand. Cans can be cut, curled, punched, pounded, painted or used as is. Tuna cans make excellent tart or pot pie pans; disposable ashtrays; or cut out the top and bottom, cover it and it makes a bracelet.

CANDLE STUBS - make excellent fire starters. Simply toss a couple of candle stubs into the kindling and light it. Candle wax is an excellent lubricant, run a stubborn saw or sticky iron with a candle stub. Stick drill bits, needles, nails or pins through a candle before using them and they will work easier. Dresser drawers slide smoother when the runners have been rubbed with candle wax.

CARDBOARD TUBES - can be used to mail something that cannot be folded. They can also be used when you need to carry a parcel tied with string. Just run the last loop across the top through a cardboard tube. Carry the package by the tube so the string won't bite into your hand and simply tear it off when you get to your destination.

EGG CARTONS - are ideal starter trays for seedlings. Punch a hole in the bottom of each cup for drainage. They can also double as ice trays when you need extra ice for parties or picnics.

OLD GLOVES - can be worn to dust furniture or a car's interior and simply throw into the washer when done.

OLD LEATHER BELTS - can be recycled into a collar for your pet.

OLD RECORDS - can be covered with tin foil and used as a disposable platter or cake plate when taking food to a potluck dinner or a bake sale.

MEAT TRAYS - us as picnic plates instead of paper; use to hold baked goods which are gifts; use as drip catchers under flower pots or paint cans.

PLASTIC BASKETS - can be refilled with berries or cherry tomatoes when you pick them from your garden. They can also be used as strainers or colanders.

PLASTIC JUGS - can be cut off at an angle so the container has a handle and can be used for toting anything; cut out the bottom and it is a megaphone; cut it diagonally from just below the handle to the base edge on the opposite side and you get a scoop for pet food or potting soil; fill it with iced tea, lemonade, fruit juices; cut off the top, below the handle and use it for paint, instead of the whole bucket; fill it with water and hang one on both ends of a broomstick to create a weight to work out with.

TOY BOX - kids can make toys out of almost anything that isn't sharp or coated with toxic paint. These discards have time-tested appeal:
- Oatmeal boxes for drums
- Thread spools for wheels on homemade vehicles
- Old magazines for project pictures or posters
- Shoe boxes for saving things
- Socks for puppets
- Buttons for necklaces
- Window shades for pull down blackboards
- Milk cartons and cardboard boxes for blocks
- Old pots and pans for rhythm instruments
- Plastic squeeze bottles for squirt guns
- Old sheets for tents and forts

All of us should take responsibility for the waste we create. This does not mean an obsessive preoccupation with everything we throw away. It simply means that we consider each discard as a potential resource, rather than automatically dismissing it as mere trash. Recycling demands an active imagination to transform a piece of junk into something wonderful and useful. It is using the ordinary in an extraordinary way. It is a way to flex our creativity, inventiveness, and resourcefulness at a very reasonable price.

Recycling is an opportunity to do something to demonstrate commitment to preserving a beautiful, healthy environment. Recycling one ton of garbage can save as much as three tons of virgin materials. Some of the benefits of recycling include:

I. Reduced costs
- recyclables can be process into saleable commodities rather than being discarded in landfills or incinerators
- recycling collection costs are much lower than garbage collection costs
- recycling trucks cost less to buy and operate than garbage collection trucks
- recycling is cheaper because dropoff is easier and quicker

II. Reduced pollution
- recycling results in less disposed materials in landfills and incinerators, resulting in less air and ground water pollution
- scrap-based manufacturing is less polluting than manufacturing from raw materials
- recycling reduces industrial energy usage

- recycling means less mining and less wear and tear on the earth

III. Community economic development
- recycling creates new businesses, jobs, increased skills and a manufacturing tax base
- recycling provides psychological and sociological benefits through individual and community feelings of accomplishment and self-reliance
- some recyclable products can be sold to recycling businesses

Summary

One of the problems which will require a creative answer is excessive waste materials. Recycling is just one step in approaching this ever increasing problem. By using the Creative Problem Solving Process, we can create alternative solutions, behaviors and incentives. As we approach the new millinium, we will be faced with even more challenges and problems created by our actions today. Recycling is just one example of creative problem solving involving personal adjustments and institutional rethinking.

Chapter 7
CREATIVITY, PLAY AND THE ARTS

Just as a plant needs rain, sun and good earth in order to attain its maximum growth, an individual needs to engage in self-expression, to gain an understanding and acceptance of self, and to become aware of the part one plays in directing one's own life in order to attain maximum growth and development. In psychology, growth theories emphasize the realization of one's full potential or the engagement of self-actualizing endeavors (Fleshman & Fryrear, 1981). The term "self-actualization" has been used by Maslow (1968) and Rogers (1962) to describe the innate human capacity to develop whatever potential lies within the individual.

This can be seen in the development of children. Children are experts in ways of learning and self-expression. They have considerable experiences in questioning, inquiring, searching, manipulating, experimenting, creating, exploring and playing. However, as children enter school, many restrictions are placed on their manipulativeness and curiosity. Schools target the cognitive and intellectual areas for development, with the areas of intuition, affect and self-expression being left to develop on their own. As a consequence, many children do not learn to express themselves or their creativity and do not learn to deal with personal difficulties in a healthy manner (Dacey, 1976).

One of the most consistent findings in creativity research with children is that discontinuities in creative development often result in loss of interest in learning, increased behavioral problems and increased emotional disturbances (Torrance, 1977a). These periods are at times so extremely stressful that an individual's creativity is inhibited, reduced or unnecessarily lost as s/he ages (Torrance, Clements & Goff, 1989). As a child ages into adulthood there are more obstacles to the development of his/her creativity and self-expressiveness. These obstacles include pressure to conform, ridicule of unusual ideas, the drive for success and rewards based on other's demands and standards, and the intolerance of a playful attitude (Dacey, 1976). It is far too common for people to grow up and lose touch with their creativity and inner potentials.

Two natural mediums for creative expression are play and art. Both are expressions created from the imagination, external representations of inner experiences and perspectives. Play and art involve the language of the imagination, the emotions, the senses and the inner self (Rossman, 1987). Sensory expression is often the only way to reach people who are in severe states of emotional withdrawal, depression or psychic confusion (McNiff, 1986). Play and art allow for the ventilation and release of negative energy and encourages creative, growth-oriented self-expression and communication.

Play

Learning is more than merely accumulating knowledge, it is also the understanding of how that knowledge can be used. Everything we learn, we learn through our senses. Therefore sensory exploration is essential for developing young children. Play is a basic form of learning by doing and a natural form of stimulation (Torrance & Goff, 1993). Play is a medium for self-expression and creative expression. Essential ingredients of play include humor, manifest joy, spontaneity and creativity.

Play is a creative process and a safe way for young children to try out, explore, experiment and fumble about with ways of learning. Creative play provides an opportunity (McCaslin, 1984):

- to develop the imagination
- for independent thinking
- for cooperation and communication
- for a healthy release of emotions
- to experience freedom of choice
- for health-engendering recreation

Play involves the imagination, active participation and freedom to invent and imitate. Much of our social learning takes place during play. Through reinforcement, modeling and instruction, children learn many of the necessary social skills by participating in group play. Play is a bonding force that satisfies the needs of the individual as well as the group.

Imaginative play develops a variety of skills and benefits the following psychosocial areas (Blatner & Blatner, 1988, p. 36):

- Personal-emotional - enhancing vitality and mental health
- Social - strengthening involvements and reducing alienation
- Educational - developing the capacity to learn more effectively, and to learn in the broadest sense of the word
- Cultural - stimulating the kind of creativity required to meet the challenges of a changing world

True play creates order, it is teamwork in which participants work closely together. Examples of play can be found in all cultures of the world and on every age level. According to McCaslin (1984, p. 5), the impulse to play can become a continuing way of learning, a medium of expression and eventually an art form.

Play is a special freedom from work and the serious nature of life. Even though the form of play may be physically strenuous or mentally demanding, the process of play is refreshing and revitalizing (Fleshman & Fryrear, 1981). The fact that play is enjoyed is one of the main reasons why it is conducive to health (Bowen & Mitchell, 1925). Play is a recognized quality of mental health and has the potential for maintaining it. There must be a balance of play and work for a healthy life.

Typically during the preschool years there are two types of play, functional and constructive:
1. functional play is manipulative play, experimenting, motor activities with and without objects; using objects in stereotypical ways; it decreases with age
2. constructive play is organized, goal-oriented play; it increases with age

There is scientific and educational evidence that play:
- increases IQ
- increases problem solving skills and abilities
- increases creativity and creative thinking skills
- increases language development
- increases social development

Many adults have an unusual definition of play and only allow themselves to "play" when they are under the influence of some mind altering substance, drugs, food or alcohol. For some reason these adults are afraid of their inner child and need some excuse, such "I was high," or "I was drunk," or "I have to eat" to justify their creative expressions. This is a dangerous situation, because it leads to lower and lower self-esteem. Adults, as well as children and youth, must be able to find healthy ways to play in order to have rich, full, joyful, productive lives. Playfulness is a healthy means of expressing ourselves and enjoying life at all ages.

The Arts

According to the National Education Association, artistic expression is a basic to an individual's intellectual, aesthetic and emotional development and therefore must be included as a component of all education. Education of the whole child cannot be accomplished unless the arts and creative expression are high priorities. According to Lowenfeld and Brittain (1970), art education may well mean the difference between a flexible creative human being and one who will not be able to apply his/her learning, who will lack inner resources, and who will have difficulty relating to his/her environment.

Art for a child is not the same as it is for an adult. For a child, art is primarily a means of expression. How they created their work of art is of much more importance than the final results or product. Technical perfection bears little relationship to self-expression, which is what creative expression is all about - the true expression of the self (Lowenfeld & Brittain, 1970).

According to Lowenfeld & Brittain (1970, p. 10), "It is only through the senses that learning can take place." It is through the senses that an individual interacts with his/her environment. Art education is the only subject matter area that truly concentrates on developing the sensory experience. Touching, seeing, hearing, smelling and tasting involve the active participation of the individual. The greater the opportunity to develop an increased sensitivity and awareness of all of the senses, the greater will be the opportunity for learning.

Art education has a special mission of developing, within the individual, those creative sensitivities that make life satisfying and meaningful. Whenever we hear a child say "I can't draw," we can be sure that some kind of interference has occurred in his/her life. The growing number of emotional and mental illnesses in this nation, along with the frightening inability to accept human beings as human beings are vivid reminders that education is failing to develop those growth attributes of individual sensibilities, spiritual well-being and the ability to live cooperatively in society.

According to Lowenfeld and Brittain (1970) art is a means of understanding the following areas of growth:
- Emotional growth - personal involvement and expression
- Physical growth - hand/eye coordination; visual and motor skills
- Perceptual growth - cultivation of the senses
- Social growth - awareness of others and their influence on life; communication of creative expression; development of cooperation skills
- Aesthetic growth - a means of organizing thinking, feeling and perceiving into an expression that communicates thoughts and feelings to someone else, such as dance or songs
- Creative growth - freedom to get involved and make choices; development of the imagination; freedom to explore, experiment and invent

Art and creativity have always been closely entwined. In art education, the final product is subordinate to the creative process. What's crucial is not the adult's answer but the child's striving toward his/her own answer.

Summary

Creativity needs to be nurtured in order for it to grow. The "anything" goes atmosphere is just as negative an influence as the authoritarian atmosphere where individuals are completely dominated. Creativity must be supported, but at the same time guided into socially acceptable channels, such as art. The best preparation for future creative action is providing people with opportunities to create using the knowledge he/she currently has.

Chapter 8
CREATIVITY, HUMOR AND WELLNESS

Our conscious and unconscious images of the future are important driving forces behind future accomplishments (Torrance, Murdock & Fletcher, 1996). Positive images of the future are powerful and magnetic forces. These images spur us on and energize us to move forward to new possibilities, solutions and achievements. Dreaming, planning and being curious about the future and wondering how much it can be influenced by our efforts are important aspects of our being human (Torrance, Murdock & Fletcher, 1996). One way of assisting us in the development of our imaginations and in the creation of positive future images is to tap and develop our creativity.

When we expand our awareness to include future possibilities we are moving beyond "what is" to explore "what might be." Our awareness shifts from facts and first impressions to multiple viewpoints, ideas and options. According to Barsky (1985), awakening a person to the life that is still burning within, to the surrounding environment and to people who we can love and be loved by in return, all represent a strong rationale for the use of the creative process as a therapeutic approach.

Creativity is certainly found in healthy children, but often gets lost as people grow up (Maslow, 1962b). The creative behavior of children can be characterized as the spirit of wonder and magic. Most healthy children have this spirit unless they have been victims of neglect, abuse, lack of love, coercive punishment or sensory deprivation (Torrance, 1963). It is natural for children to learn in creative ways and by the time they enter school, they already have a variety of learning skills.

Children are experts in creative ways of learning and if they learn to suppress or neglect their creative potentials, then when faced with stress as adults, they will most likely not refer to or rely upon their creative abilities to deal with stress. At the same time, if our creative potentials are encouraged and developed throughout childhood, then in adulthood when we are faced with stress, we will most likely rely on our creative abilities, our inner strengths to deal with stress.

Stress and the harmful effects of stress have received much attention in medical and psychological professions. Many effective interventions have used imagery and humor to relieve the harmful effects of stress. Maslow (1959) stated that creativity is a kind of intellectual play which gives us permission to be ourselves, to fantasize, to let loose and to experience personal freedom. Humor is a fun way to relieve stress and enjoy life.

Humor

Humor is creative. We listen as we are led down a path to a surprise ending, something different than we thought would happen - a change in thinking. An optical illusion is much the same way only visual. We see one image and then another images comes out. Being able to switch perspectives requires flexible thinking which is an a spect of creative thinking.

Without humor, life would be unbearable to most people. Humor is an interaction of psychological, physiological and social processes. Humor weakens the bonds of conformity, allowing for spontaneous and flexible behavior. People use humor as survival techniques and as healing forces. Humor serves as the social function of promoting group membership and helps us deal with awkward moments in a positive, memorable way, such as uncontrollably laughing at a wedding or a funeral.

Almost all definitions of humor include elements of surprise, unusual combinations and unusual ways of looking at things. Producing or "having a sense of humor" is an important creative strength. Humor is a good liberator, it frees thought and suspends the rules of time, place, logic and conduct. Humor has the capacity to relax tensions, provide outlets for otherwise unacceptable behavior or impulses and puts an individual in a frame of mind more conducive to effective interchanges with others.

Humor is one of the most effective forms of communication. It dissolves tension, provides essential breaks in conversations, disarms aggression, makes criticism more palatable, and emphasizes a point of view. Humor radiates us, makes us feel happy, gives us joyful illuminations, and gives us insights into the absurdities and interesting disharmonies of all aspects of human life. It brings people together, builds confidence, and leads to positive, creative exchanges.

Playfulness is characteristic of highly creative people (Cropley, 1990). An atmosphere of play usually contributes to humor and laughter. Highly creative people have been found to initiate humor more often, to place greater value on having a sense of humor, to appreciate and understand others' humor more and to be playful verbally when interacting with others (Cornett, 1986). Humor is liberating. It has the power to release us from the many inhibitions and restrictions under which we live our daily lives.

According to Ziv (1980), humor can best be understood as a creative act. The very act of producing humor is creativity in itself (Robinson, 1991). Correlational studies have indicated that significant relationships exist between humor and creativity (Ziv, 1983). According to Koestler (1964), the type of thinking involved in creating humor is identical to that required for scientific, literary, artistic and other forms of creative activities.

There are numerous reports, both in professional literature and in folklore, of persons who have been cured, or at least eased, in numerous medical and/or psychological conditions, by the use of laughter and humor (Moody, 1978). Studies focusing on the relationship between sense of humor and health have been rare, but the research that has been done supports the view that humor is positively related to healthy adjustment. Positive attitudes and a healthy sense of humor help people adjust to stressful situations, changes, losses and prevent these stressors from manifesting into physical and/or psychological disorders (Klein, 1989). Humor is a valuable resource to help people adjust to difficult and painful situations.

According to McGhee (1979), the possession of a good sense of humor is commonly assumed to be necessary for good mental health. Twenty seconds of laughing gives the heart the same workout as three minutes of hard rowing (Klein, 1989). A good laugh makes us feel better by:
- increasing oxygen in the blood
- exercising the lungs, diaphragm, face muscles and sometimes even arms and legs (knee slapping, high 5's)
- slowing pulse; decreasing tensions; and increasing the production of endorphins, the body's natural painkillers.

Nurturing and rewarding humor will encourage its development. Using humor to boost the morale of students usually has a positive effect on their learning (Hill, 1988). One way to facilitate humor is to allow for free, uninhibited expression of original connections. This can be accomplished by deferring judgment and creating a relaxed, "safe" atmosphere for creative and humorous expressions. Humor can serve the very important function of opening the doors to an open, spontaneous, flexible and generally healthy interaction with others (McGhee, 1979). Specialists in many fields, including psychology, education, medicine and business, have promoted humor on the basis of its value in fostering good mental health and wellness (Hill, 1988).

Wellness

According to the World Health Organization, health is a state of complete physical, mental and social well-being and is not merely the absence of disease and infirmity. This implies that health is more than obtaining care for malfunctions, and requires an awareness of the whole body, of its components and processes working together (Torrance, Clements and Goff, 1989). Medical science has primarily focused on an individual with little regard for the mind of that same individual. Psychology, the science of the mind, has generally limited its research to the rational and quantifiable aspects of disease or illness oriented thoughts and behaviors.

As early as 1907, Dubois wrote about the influence of the mind over the body. However, due to Freud's early view of the unconscious and the dominance of behavioristic and experimental psychology, we generally have accepted the self-limiting ideas of being powerless to control or change events in our bodies and lives (Green & Green, 1977). Science, for the most part, has been a search for explanations in terms of complex structures built of small measurable units, yet some things that happen to real people in the real world just do not fit into well-established categories (Borysenko, 1988).

According to Ornstein and Sobel (1987), the brain minds the body in terms of the function of internal organs, the safety and stability of the individual and the maintenance of health. An examples of this is the placebo effect. Individuals who have taken placebos when they believed they were taking a healing medication often show decreases in pain, nausea, anxiety, and even tumor cells (Achterberg, 1985). There is not only a change in their attitudes but also a change in their biochemistry. The importance of the placebo is that it gives credence to the idea that humans possess certain self-healing mechanisms which are activated by altering the images or expectancies in regard to health. Altering these images requires creativity.

Psychoneuroimmunology is an emerging science that investigates the roles of imagery, the mind, and their effects on the health of an individual. According to Green and Green (1977), every change in the physiological state is accompanied by a change in the mental-emotional state. There appears to be a rich and intricate communication system linking the mind, the immune system, our beliefs and images which can affect the body's ability to defend itself (Borysenko, 1988). If we expand our belief system to include the concept that the mind and the body are intricately interconnected and changes in either effects both, then it becomes apparent that there are no diseases that are purely physical or purely mental.

Researchers have demonstrated that humans can develop conscious control over their internal states. Green and Green (1977) reported a remarkable study on Yogiraja Vaidijaraga, in which he demonstrated a significant lowering of the metabolic rate. He was placed in an airtight box containing about 60 cubic feet of air. In 90 minutes, a lit candle inside of this box went out due to lack of oxygen. He stayed in the box for 6 more hours.

He demonstrated the power of the mind and the body in a relaxed state. In a relaxed state, there is decreased oxygen consumption, decreased respiration, decreased heart rate, predominance of alpha rhythms (relaxed state of mind), decreased blood pressure, decreased muscle tension and increased flow in cerebral blood vessels (Korn & Johnson, 1983). When we are relaxed, not only is our body relaxed, but also our mind is relaxed and free from worry or anxiety.

Worry and anxiety can be health-threatening images created by the mind in response to stress. These images are beneficial when they enable us to survive in a potentially harmful situation. However, if this "alarm stage" of stress response is prolonged, it becomes distress and becomes harmful (Selye, 1974). Stress and its negative impact on health occur as a result of a mismatch between perceived demands and perceived resources. According to Rossman (1987, p. 36), uncontrolled imagination gives humans the unique ability to compress a lifetime of stress into every passing moment.

Imagery

The communication between the mind and body occurs in mental dialogues called images. Imagery is the flow of thoughts or perceptions with which we can hear, see, taste, smell and feel. An image is an inner representation of our experiences and our dreams - a way in which our minds code, store and express information. It is the language of the imagination, the emotions and of the deep self (Rossman, 1987).

There is a rich history of the use of imagery in behavioral and social science research. The Simonton's (1984) found that a person's active imagination can aid a patient in curing his/her own cancer. Through the use of imagery, cancer patients have reduced and destroyed tumors. Midwives have long used imagery and relaxation exercises to help women in labor to control pain, diminish fear and release tension. One very interesting study in the uses of imagery was conducted by Willard (1977). This study demonstrated the effectiveness of imagery and hypnotic states of consciousness to increase breast size. Over a 12 week period, 85% of the participants were aware of a significant increase and 46% had to increase their bra size.

Unfortunately our culture has not valued the importance of everyday imagination and as a result, imagery is often equated with the fanciful, the unreal, the impractical and sometimes even dangerous. However, there is considerable evidence that various forms of imagery can alter psychophysiological functioning in the direction of increased health, relieving the effects of prolonged stress, reducing states of hyperarousal and restoring the body's natural ability to ward off disease through the immune system (Pelletier, 1977).

It is important to realize that each person's imagery varies as much as their fingerprints just as most of us vary in the amount of development of each of our senses. Although our images are a product of all of our senses, most of us rely more heavily on one certain sense than on the others. For example, some of us remember how a situation felt, or what we heard, said, tasted or otherwise experienced. Our hopes and fears are the internal representations of our images. Whereas art, dance, inventions and other forms of creative expression are the external representations of our images, our perspectives, our interpretations.

Everyone has the ability to imagine. Some of us forget to use our imaginations and this ability atrophies. Some of us, however, have nurtured our imaginations and experience very vivid images. And some of us do not realize we are using our imaginations when we mentally rehearse a sales presentation or an obstacle course. Yet these rehearsals evoke muscular changes, increased blood pressure, brain wave changes and sweat glands even become active (Achterberg, 1985).

Mental images are not only effective motivational tools for recovering health, but also important tools for self-discovery and for making creative changes in other areas of our lives. An important use of imagery is in the creation of positive future images.

Enlarged, enriched and more accurate images of the future positively influence our abilities to adapt, cope and grow in an ever changing society. Our future images aid us in our search for identity and self-understanding. Creativity researchers have recognized the connection between creativity and images of the future for some time.

When we expand our awareness to include future possibilities, we are moving beyond "what is" to explore "what might be." Our awareness shifts from facts and first impressions to multiple viewpoints, ideas and options. We become more creative, more open to possibilities and more self-actualized.

Summary

Illness is not purely a physical problem but a problem of the whole person which includes not only the body, but also the mind and the emotions. Mental imagery and relaxation techniques have been used to help patients learn to believe in their ability to contribute to their recovery. Humor and imagery can be very powerful tools in mobilizing the resources of the mind and the body to combat illness. By developing our creativity, we will be better able to develop the positive future images necessary for healthy, self-actualized living.

Wellness involves the physical (body) and mental (mind) health of an individual, positive future images and true communications with ourselves and others. Creativity, humor and imagery are essential ingredients in the maintenance of healthy mind/body communications, for the reduction of pain and stress as well as providing motivation and fuel for future goals, accomplishments and achievements. Creative expression arouses the adventurous spirit within and creates a zest for living. Valuing and developing our creativity will raise our levels of wellness (Dun, 1961; Torrance, 1978a)

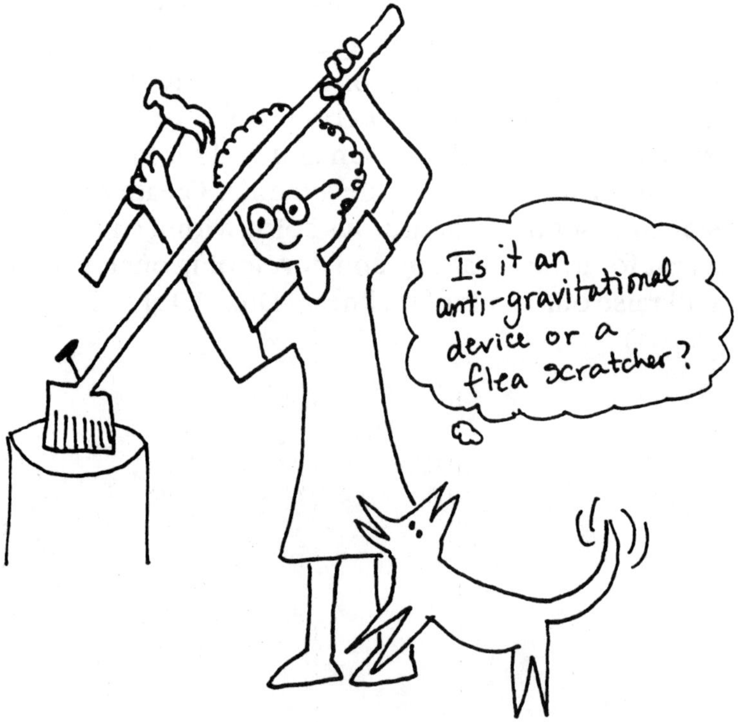
Is it an
anti-gravitational
device or a
flea scratcher?

Chapter 9
INVENTING AND FUTURISTICS

Today's young people, who represent our next wave of intellectual enthusiasm and achievement, are a reminder that we can ill afford to cling to old technologies and rigid ways of thinking. New ideas and new technologies will lead this country to success in the 21st century.

In research conducted by Torrance from 1960-1965, he found that girls at the second and third grade level needed encouragement to cultivate their inventiveness. He concluded that factors causing the scarcity of women among inventors and creative scientists begin operating as early as second or third grade. According to Torrance (1995a), the social sanctions against highly creative boys, who appear more feminine, and highly creative girls, who seem more masculine, may cause children to sacrifice their creativity at this early age. Creativity, by it nature, requires both sensitivity and independence.

A report by the American Association of University Women in 1995, cited the absence of attention to girls in the current educational debate which suggests that girls and boys have identical educational experiences in school. Nothing could be further from the truth. There is clear evidence that the educational system is not meeting girls' needs.

From this report, we know that all of us have felt the lack of teacher attention, we are less apt to relate to materials we studied than boys and we were not encouraged or expected to pursue higher-level math and science courses. If someone paid attention to our learning it was usually someone in our family or a mentor. They were crucial to our creative development. Occasionally, we had a teacher who encouraged us to love learning, but these instances were more rare than abundant (McCracken, 1997). Consequently, we know little about the accomplishments of women and have few role models to emulate.

Women and men must participate equally in problem solving efforts, opportunities and responsibilities if we, as a nation, are to work to our full potential. In 1993, only 8% of patents granted to Americans were to women. Human creativity has and will continue to determine our future and it's time to include women as equal partners in determining that future.

Women Inventors

American settlers had to be extremely inventive and creative to survive and build communities in the wilderness. Great women, who have overcome enormous social obstacles, have made contributions that have changed our lives.

Sybilla Masters and her husband, Thomas, bought a mill in 1714 (Showell & Amram, 1995). Their problem was how to convince colonists to use their gristmill and not one closer to their homes. Sybilla came up with the answer: To produce a better, finer quality flour by improving the machinery used in cleaning and processing the grain. Sybilla's invention used pestles or mallets to crush the grain instead of grinding it with a flat stone. Sybilla was granted a patent on her invention by King George in the name of her husband Thomas (since a married woman was property which legally belonged to her husband).

During the eighteenth and nineteenth centuries, women were educated differently than men. Women were trained in manners and morals of polite society and in the care of the home and children. Men studied science, technology, and politics. Social pressures kept most women from stepping out of traditional roles. A woman inventor needed a great deal of self-confidence to ignore being called immoral for going against tradition. People expected a woman, even if she was a genius, to remain true to the traditional image of a mother and a wife (Moussa, 1991).

The Patent Act of 1790 was silent on gender thus offering women the same patenting privileges as men. The first woman to be granted a patent was Mary Kies in 1809 for a straw-weaving process (Macdonald, 1992).

During the 1800's, most women's lives were filled with long, hard hours of chores: washing, cleaning, cooking and raising kids. If a woman took time to invent something, it was usually a way to ease her burden or make extra money. Typical inventions by women were churns for making butter, bee-keeping equipment and improved cook stoves.

The Civil War marked a turning point for women inventors. The war called men away from farms, shops and factories, leaving women to carry on. If something broke down, the woman had to repair it. In many cases the woman was responsible for the family business as well as the household. These survival experiences built confidence in women who discovered that they were handy with machines and capable of solving problems using technology. Women discovered that when they were needed to do "men's work" they did it well.

Clarissa Britain, of Michigan, received patents for seven inventions (Showell & Amram, 1995). Her 1863 patent was for an Improvement to Ambulances. It was used to transport wounded men from battlefield to a hospital without having to move them from a stretcher.

Helen Blanchard was the daughter of a prominent shipbuilder in Maine who died and left her with no money (Showell & Amram, 1995). Fortunately, she was not only mechanically talented but also persistent. She began tinkering with sewing machines, figuring out improvements that were new and useful and would earn her money. She borrowed money for her first patent application. She eventually received 24 patents for improvements on sewing machines or attachments. She did so well on royalties from the use of her inventions and her own sewing machine business she was able to buy back the family homestead, which had been lost when her father's business had failed.

Often when women entered the world of technology, they were ignored because it was unbelievable that women had anything valuable to offer. Consequently, Margaret Knight had a hard time convincing men in the 1870s that she understood her own inventions (Showell & Amram, 1995). Knight had a lifelong interest in technology. In her youth, she worked in a cotton mill which led her to develop a device to make looms safer. Before the 1870s, almost everything was packaged in wood, tin or fabric. Margaret became interested in paper bags which were shaped like envelopes and could not hold very much. The ones with flat bottoms were folded and glued by hand, a tedious process. Knight spent months working out her ideas for a machine that would make square-bottomed bags. She was granted a patent in 1871.

Sarah Breedlove Walker was born on a plantation in Louisiana to former slaves (Showell & Amram, 1995). She picked cotton, became a washerwoman, was promoted to cook and from there promoted herself into the business of manufacturing hair goods and preparations.

Sarah Breedlove thought that her hair was lifeless and hard to manage. None of the products for sale seemed to improve her hair. She began experimenting with different mixtures of herbs and lotions until she created a lotion that made her hair glossy and healthy-looking. She began selling this lotion to other women and hired women to sell it in the best neighborhoods.

Sarah married a newspaperman, Charles Walker and together they created the Madam C. J. Walker Manufacturing Company. They sold Sarah Walker's own inventions: hair lotions and creams for black women and an improved hairstyling hot comb. Her inventions helped her launch a business empire. She built a factory to make her products and traveled around the country setting up beauty salons where her products were used and sold. Women who worked in the salons were given special training.

By 1918, Madam Walker had become the first American self-made woman millionaire. She set up special schools around the country to teach black women how to care for their hair and skin and how to become teachers themselves. She sold her own products and developed a whole network of saleswomen who traveled door-to-door to introduce customers to the new products. The door-to-door system and hairstyling lessons became the keys to her empire. Walker's methods have been adopted by many other businesses around the world.

During World Wars I and II, women pitched in to replace the men who were called away from factories, laboratories, hospitals and other businesses. Women helped the war efforts in many ways by inventing many defense-related devices, such as the automatic pistol, a bomb-launching device, a rear sight for guns, the mine, percussion and ignition fuses, railway torpedoes, etc.

An important and lasting effect of the two world wars was that women were able to break into new fields. Highly trained women could work in factories, research laboratories and other businesses that had been off limits before the wars. During the 1950's about one and a half percent of patents were in a woman's name. However, since the 1960's, the number of women applying for patents has increased every year with the number of patents being issued to women in 1993 being at about 8 percent of all of the patents issued.

Sometimes an inventor will choose to give up any profits so that an invention can reach the public. This was true for chemist Rachel Fuller Brown and microbiologist Elizabeth Lee Hazen of the New York State Department of Health (Showell & Amram, 1995). They worked together for several years to find a cure for fungal infections. Hazen and Brown looked at soil samples from all over the world, searching for a bacterium that could destroy fungi. They found this bacterium and created a medicine that they named nystatin.

Nystatin was a major medical breakthrough because it kills the fungus without harming the essential bacteria in the body that control fungi. It had no bad side effects. Brown and Hazen had strong feelings about how the drug should be developed and used. If they gave up the patent rights to their employer, they would have no say in the drug's development, marketing and use. However, as individuals, they did not have the money to patent and test the drug.

Fortunately, the two researchers got help from the Research Corporation, which had been set up to help the public benefit from scientific research. The Research Corporation took care of the patent application for Brown and Hazen, produced the drug in large quantities in order to conduct the necessary tests to prove it worked. The process of approval for nystatin took 5 years.

The patent was granted to Brown and Hazen who agreed to assign all their royalties to the Research Corporation. To get nystatin on the market, the Research Corporation licensed it to E. R. Squibb and Sons to make and sell for five years. Royalties received by the Research Corporation during in the life of the patent was more than 13 million dollars. Half of the money went to support research and the other half went to establish the Brown-Hazen Fund to support biomedical research.

Nystatin has proven useful in destroying fungi that attack trees, keeps certain foods, such as bananas, from spoiling and has been used to restore valuable paintings damaged by mold.

Today there continues to be an unequal ratio of successful women to men in creative fields. The creativity world is largely a man's world (Piirto, 1991) dominated by research conducted by men using criteria appropriate for men based on male needs and logic. Inventing has been primarily considered a "male" field, yet female inventors do exist.

All kinds of people can and do invent. The idea that one's gender somehow precludes the possibility of pursuing any technological endeavor is not only outdated but also dangerous (Vare & Ptacek, 1987, p. 17). The world cannot afford to neglect the talents of half of its people if solutions to the many problems that face us are to be discovered.

Finding Ideas

The study of inventions involves interdisciplinary studies and the exploration of science with a purpose. Learners need opportunities to see concrete applications of scientific principles which they get by studying and experiencing the inventing process. Inventions are such a significant part of our lives that its difficult to imagine any subjects taught in today's schools which do not have direct ties to the broad topics of inventing, inventions and inventors (Flack, 1989).

Recyclables, garage sales and flea markets provide a bonanza of raw materials for inventors to use in creating models or prototypes of their ideas. It is easier to use existing parts and materials and it makes the prototype easier to reproduce. For example, in one of our games, we needed a one minute timer. They are not easy to find. We searched and searched. Finally, we found a whole game parts manufacturer who would sell us one minute timers by the gross (144 pieces). We didn't need that many, but at least we found what we needed!

Our searches have taken us to hardware stores, auto parts stores, lumber yards, marine and boat supplies stores, medical supply businesses, sporting goods stores, tractor and truck supplies stores, toy stores, pet stores, fabric shops, trading posts, different towns and cities, almost anywhere you can imagine. Persistence is the key to inventing! Einstein said, "Genius is 1% inspiration and 99% perspiration." He was so right!

After the prototype is built and your idea works, then it is time to conduct an extensive investigation of what's already out on the market. Is there anything like your idea already out there? If so, is your idea a significant improvement? This will also require investigation. We went to over a dozen hardware stores looking for one of our ideas to see if it was already a commercial product. The investigation also includes asking people if they have ever heard of your idea before and do they think it would be something they would sell or that people would buy.

Asking experts about your invention is another way to learn more about the marketability of your idea. A nearby college, university, the Internet, the library are great resources for information. People who work in the field are important "everyday" experts to talk with as well since they will be using your invention if it is marketable. The more information you have on the market you will sell to the better.

It is also very important for you to admit to people right up front that this is not your expertise and that you would like their advice or thoughts on your idea.

Sometimes their remarks are hard to take, but don't get defensive, just listen and learn from what they are telling you. As you are talking with people, you will hear the same comment. If you hear the same thing over and over, then believe it and decide what to do about it. At this point you can determine if you want to move forward with this idea or move to another one.

So how do you get another idea? One way is to ask around and see what people say is a problem for them. Benjamin Franklin listened to the complaints of his neighbors, acquaintances, family, etc. and invented what they complained about. Choose one of these problems and brainstorm ways to solve it until one solution stands out from the rest. Sketch or write down your solution. Then build a working model or prototype and see how it works. If you think you have a really good idea, then you need to protect it by filing a disclosure document with the U.S. Patent and Trademark Office, Washington, DC 20231.

There are state and local inventors groups who meet to support each other and to promote inventing. They can be an excellent source for speakers and resources. Many states have U.S. Patent and Trademark Depository Libraries where you can do an initial patent search at no or minimal cost. Many colleges, universities, businesses have employees who are inventors or courses/programs on inventing. These resources could be made available to learners through collaborative programs between public and private institutions and organizations.

Schools, neighborhoods and communities could host inventions fairs where inventors young and old display and demonstrate their ideas. With corporate sponsorship, the winners could receive scholarships or assistance in patenting their ideas. Communities could sponsor a young inventor for a small, percentage of the invention/idea or sponsor an inventors workshop with space, tools and access to the necessary expertise to develop, manufacture and distribute new products. The inventors, workers and community could all profit from the sale of the new products, thus rewarding and promoting inventing and entrepreneurship.

Inventing Women

Women can help other women by sharing our stories, expertise and experiences. We can be contributors to the empowerment of the female voice. The female voice has been silenced by tradition and a culture that has expected women to be seen, but not heard. We know through the study of creativity that a key element is communicating the idea. It is no wonder then that women only represent 8% of those who receive patents, because filing a patent application requires communication of the invention to another, usually a man.

In order for the creative voice of wommen to be heard, we must know more about it. To address this issue of voice, a new association for women interested in creativity has been started. TCAW (The Creativity Association for Women) is a new Internet site for women to connect and network regarding their creativity. Dr. McCracken and myself started TCAW to further our research into and support of the creativity of women. The plans are to produce a bi-monthly newsletter and an annual conference on the creativity of women. To join via the Internet go to:

www.cowboy.net/~mcgoff/

Inventing Process

My inventing partner and I mentor each other constantly. Together, we have become productive inventors, apart, we know we would not be inventors. Our style is a feminine style of cooperation and collaboration for mutually beneficial outcomes. As women, we nurture each other's ideas and dreams by helping each other reach her goals and realize her dreams. Women listen to each other, respect each others' ideas and provide constructive feedback when working collaboratively.

Getting the initial idea is like an engine getting a spark to start, it sets off a series of reactions and sequences of events. If you don't have a spark, the engine won't run, but the spark is only the first step of an engine runnning. Once an idea is communicated it is then time to brainstorm about it. What are pros and cons, develop a design and build a model to see if the idea works.

After careful consideration, we decide whether or not to continue with the idea. Costs, feasibility, marketability, time, etc. are all discussed in determining whether or not to proceed with an idea. If the decision to proceed is made, then we design an action plan to determine what to do next and a timeline for completing each step. From here a working prototype is developed.

Personal Examples

Communicating your idea for a new invention is somewhat of an obstacle. It takes time and patience

INVENTING AND FUTURISTICS

for the development and refinement of a working prototype. For example, we created a life-saving rescue device for getting people down stairs when the elevators shut down due to fire. Initially we thought that, due to the Americans with Disabilities Act, more people with disabilities will be working in high rise buildings. Our next thought was how are these people going to get out of these buildings when the elevators shut down due to fire?

First, we built a model using a piece of tupperware and a small bear strapped into the tupperware with shoe strings. We set up some bricks to act like stairs and pushed the LifeSled down the stairs. It worked. We then met with a mechanical engineer to get the blueprints drawn. We entered the drawings in a statewide competition for inventors and it won first place in the adult division. At that competition, we met a man who said he would loan us the seed money we needed to build the prototype and get a patent.

We found a plastics manufacturer to build our LifeSled prototype. It took about 4 weeks for him to build the first model. We then took it out and tested it up and down a variety of stairs. We went back and forth making modifications for some time. It is essential that the inventors test the invention to see if it works as it was designed to work.

After we completed our testings of the LifeSled and were satisfied with it, we began entertaining ideas for what to do next. After we received the patent, which takes some time, we tried to sell the idea to manufacturers in the rescue business. We received rejection after rejection. Companies are very hesitant to take submissions from outside. Many companies have research and development departments to do their inventing work.

After a couple of years of no success, we felt the LifeSled was a good enough idea to proceed with self-manufacturing. We raised some money by selling percentages of the LifeSled to family members. We hired a designer to streamline the LifeSled into a commercially viable product which was renamed, the LifeSlider. He made us a mold so we could manufacture them. This designer knew a potential investor and manufacturer. This investor eventually purchased the patent and we are now receiving a royalty on each LifeSlider sold. If you would like more information on the LifeSlider, contact them at 316-442-4543 or fax 316-442-2320.

Another invention of ours is the Turtle Shells protective sports bra. This idea came to us while we were playing racquetball and got hit in the chest by the ball. It really hurt, so we went to sporting goods stores to see about buying a protective bra to prevent such pain. We found out that there was no such thing available. So we began experimenting with different types of bras. We made the first one out of leather. This created a problem, because we couldn't find anyone to sew the leather bras. Next, we thought about inserts to put into a pocket in the bra for protection. It took numerous tries to perfect the idea, but finally we created something we were comfortable with and proceeded with a patent search.

We found that no one had patented such a product for women playing contact sports. Over the course of several years, we have received a utility patent, a design patent, a trademark and another utility patent is pending on Turtle Shells.

INVENTING AND FUTURISTICS

The next hurdle was raising the money to produce and sell the product. Through the use of numerous credit cards and investments by family members and friends, the Turtle Shells protective sports bra with protective cups is commercially available. For more information, contact the YESS Corporation at 800-999-0927, fax 405-748-6613 or via Internet at http://www.turtle-shells.com

Inventing Tidbits

- Where do ideas come from?
  - They come when anyone is willing to seek them out.
- Creative ideas can happen when one idea is picked up from one place, another idea from another place and when the two are combined a new idea is formed.
- Creative ideas are rarely new, they're just old concepts combined in new and useful ways, such as the electric screwdriver.
  - Benjamin Franklin made the first bifocal glasses by combining two lenses in one pair of glasses.
  - Alexander Graham Bell combined his knowledge of the human ear with his knowledge of magnetism and electricity.
- Find a need and set your mind to work on it.
- Need is the mother of invention. When a need is determined, someone sets out to fill it.
  - A farmer had to stop his work in the hayfield to go to the house to wash the clothes for his sick wife. He'd never washed clothes before and was surprised at what a back breaking job it was. Finally tiring of the

whole thing, he set his mind to work and developed the mechanical washing machine.

- Fred Smith noticed that some businesses had a need for overnight delivery of their packages. He formed a company that specialized in that service, called it Federal Express, and became a multimillionaire.

- Remember - knowing too much about a particular thing can overload the circuits and reduce creativity. Regulate input, incubate.
- Creative people are playful people. The Chinese invented the rocket as a toy for little children.
- The human mind is like a muscle. If we don't use it, we lose it. To develop the ability to produce good ideas, we have to exercise our brains. Don't let other people do your creative thinking for you - such as TV and video games.
- The key to your own creative future is sitting right between your ears. Use it!
- You'd think most of the great developments of the world came through skilled people trained in their field. This is not the case. The trained people are many times too close to the problem to see the real solution.

- Kodachrome film was developed by a musician.

- The automatic telephone was developed by an undertaker.

- Louis Pasteur was not an M.D.

- The Wright Brothers were bike mechanics, not aeronautical engineers.

- It takes creative *effort* to product creative results.
- Some of the greatest creativity comes from nature. Whenever you are faced with a difficult problem,

INVENTING AND FUTURISTICS

look to nature to see how it solved the same kind of problem.
- Camouflage has been used by all kinds of creatures for thousands of years. Military personnel thought of copying the approach to hide tanks, trucks and soldiers.
- The hypodermic needle is patterned after a rattlesnake fang.
- Velcro was invented by a Swiss engineer who observed a burr that grabbed onto his clothing and would not let go.
- The jet airplane uses propulsion to travel through the air much like a squid uses it in water.

- "Ah, Ha!" ideas come as flashes of unexpected insight, as bolts out of the blue. Usually they come after the conscious mind has ceased work on the problem, allowing the subconscious to work on it. This time is called *incubation*.
- The ability to ask questions is the most important of all creative skills. When we don't ask questions, nothing happens.
- Often finding the right solution to a problem may be as simple as asking the right question.
- Good key words to include in questions are:
  Who?   Why?   How?   What?
  When? Where? Which? So What?
  Well?
- Unique ideas are resisted. It takes courage and persistence to bring them to reality.
- Fear is the biggest barrier to creativity. It locks the mind up and won't let it work.
- Habits also kill creativity. Roads too often traveled turn into ruts.

- The ability to be creative is not confined to any one group or type of person. Anyone can be creative. All that is required is the *desire* to make it happen and the *willingness* to put in the necessary effort.
- Only by knowing the real problem can you ever find a solution.
- It usually takes a good deal of time to bring an ideas to the public. For example, from the initial idea to selling it was:
  - 30 years for antibiotics
  - 30 years for the zipper
  - 22 years for instant coffee
  - 7 years for the ballpoint pen
- Edgar Allan Poe submitted *The Raven* to more than 40 publishers before it was finally printed.
- Thomas Edison went through over 1,000 types of filaments before he finally found one that worked for his light bulb.
- In order for a creative idea to be financially successful, it must first be useful.
- One of the most vital of all creative approaches is to use the image in the mind to create something in reality.
- Mozart composed entire scores inside his head.
- According to Albert Einstein, "Imagination is more important than knowledge."
- The more real you can make your idea, the more successful you will be in selling it to others. Build a prototype, a model, to test your idea. Convert the idea into something that can be experienced by all of the senses.
- A lot of people have ideas, but few decide to do something about them. Creativity is action.

- Minds are like parachutes, they only function when open.

Futuristics

Futuristics is the examination of future alternatives and possible results before they are put into action. The future is being made today (Torrance, 1980). By examining the trends of yesterday and today, many characteristics of the future can be forecast. Studying the future encourages learners to think more creatively about future possibilities and the impact of present actions on the future, such as:
- problems of pollution worldwide
- pressures on food supplies and hunger
- finiteness of nonrenewable natural resources
- adequate housing and living spaces
- ecological concerns and conservation
- consumption and distribution of world resources

Futurism is the study of alternatives and understanding change. At the first World Conference on Gifted Children, Torrance (1976) cited reasons for the study of the future:
- an increased rate of change
- future careers in occupations that do not now exist
- choices being made today determine the future
- today's children are the future
- curiosity about the future

It is through their images of the future that learners determine what they will be motivated to learn. Positive and healthy images of the future influence our ability to live, cope, adjust and grow in a constantly changing world.

Four essential characteristics of future studies are (Torrance, 1978b):
1) opportunities to think creatively and to be creatively expressive
2) interdisciplinary studies and activities
3) lots of practice in teams; skills must be practiced to be of any use
4) future oriented topics of interest and concern to the learners

Futures Instructional Strategies

A part of the Future Problem Solving Program, is the future scenario writing contest. According to Torrance (1980), a scenario is a creative tool for exploring and forecasting possible futures. It is a description of a sequence of events that might possibly happen in the future. Scenarios are usually developed by studying the facts as they are now and imagining a variety of possible outcomes that might occur. The scenario provides a methodology for taking knowledge - such as hard science, trend analyses, Delphi studies, cross-impact analyses - and shaping it into a creative narrative.

A future scenario is a short story describing how the future may be affected by current trends and issues. Although the scenario is a forecast of the future, it is written as if it is happening today. A future scenario revolves around a problem solving focus on: 1) discovering or proposing a solution, 2) possible consequences of not pursuing a solution, or 3) possible consequences of implementing a particular solution. The purpose of the scenario is not to simply illustrate a possible future world, but to involve the reader in a constructive examination of desirable futures (Torrance, 1975b).

The objective of futures education is to make the future as psychologically real as possible (Torrance, 1980). Acting out future scenarios is another approach to studying the future. This method is called future problem solving sociodrama.

This method involves having people act out meaningful situations as they may appear in the future. The effectiveness of this procedure depends upon significance and relevance of the situation for the group and the extent to which they are able to project themselves into the future (Torrance, 1980).

Sociodrama uses dramatic techniques to produce and test alternative solutions in groups. It is an effective instructional methodology as well as group problem solving process (Torrance, Murdock & Fletcher, 1995). Sociodrama is more than role playing. It is a creative approach to problems and a natural way of projecting into the future. Sociodrama requires action, reaction and interaction.

Sociodrama differs from psychodrama in that people play a stereotypical role in sociodrama and play themselves in psychodrama. Sociodramatic play can be directed to attain therapeutic as well as learning goals. As a problem solving tool, sociodrama has been used from the classroom to the boardroom. Sociodrama can be used to:
- understand and resolve problems or conflicts in the future
- provide practice in carrying out action
- increase awareness and clarity of attitudes and perceptions

- provide training in future leadership or cooperative roles
- provide practice in planning and implementing decisions
- develop a greater understanding of different values, feelings, perceptions of others
- assist in the discovery and development of personal strengths
- identify gaps in information and skills

Summary

The ability to solve problems creatively is fundamental for inventing and studying the future. According to Kauffman (1976), the biggest single failing in thinking about the future is a failure to be sufficiently imaginative about what might happen. A fertile imagination is a requirement for creativity, inventing and future problem solving.

EXCELLENT RESOURCE:
World Future Society
7910 Woodmont Ave., Suite 450
Bethesda, MD 20897-1405

Chapter 10
CREATIVITY AND MENTORING

The term "mentor" seems to have originated from Homer's epic, The Odyssey. Before Ulysses embarked on his ten year adventure, he chose his wise and trusted friend (Mentor) to guard, guide, and teach his son. This model of mentorship has not changed much over time. Those who have guarded, guided, taught, and counseled persons in such relationships have varying labels in other cultures and periods of history. We have had "sponsor," "master," "guru," "sensei," "patron," "coach," and so on.

The term "mentor" is the term which seems to have been generally accepted in the United States. Mentors are usually influential people (advantaged) who significantly help others (disadvantaged) to reach their life goals. Mentors have the power to promote anothers welfare, training, learning, and/or careers.

Mentors are usually identified as having outstanding knowledge, skills and expertise in a particular area. Mentoring is the experience of "taking someone under your wing." It is believing in the potential of another and helping them get where they want to go.

Importance of Mentoring

Mentors serve as wise and trusted counselors concerned with mental health, full mental functioning, educational achievement, and vocational success. Torrance (1984) presents evidence that mentors clearly do make a difference. Men and women with mentors completed more education than those without mentors. It might be argued that the more education people acquire, the better the chances of finding mentors. Having a mentor is a significant factor in adult creative achievement for both men and women (Torrance, 1984).

Mentors legitimize experiential and manipulative learning as well as learning by trial and error. Mentors encourage mentees to play with problems and dilemmas, look at possible solutions from various viewpoints, let one thing lead to another and assist the mentee in creating visions and future images. What could be more important in today's ever changing world than assisting creative individuals in realizing their potential and productively contributing to society.

Mentor Relationships

A mentor encourages and supports the mentee in expressing and testing ideas and in thinking things through, regardless of his/her own views. The mentor protects the mentee from reactions of his/her peers long enough for the mentee to try out some of his/her ideas and modify them. The mentor keeps the situation open enough so that originality can occur and persist.

Frequently, the mentee's ideas are far ahead of his/her peers and s/he possesses an unusually strong urge to communicate his/her ideas and results of testing those ideas. The mentor is a "sounding board" who genuinely respects the questions and ideas of the mentee. This support stimulates further explorations and imagination.

A mentor supports a mentee by looking for opportunities for the mentee to grow and be rewarded for that growth. The mentor's networks provide him/her with information on certain opportunities such as scholarships, awards, grants, jobs, etc. It must be understood, however, that being aware of an opportunity does not guarantee the mentee success.

Mentor relationships often require flexibility and a sense of humor to successfully negotiate problems which will arise in developing a caring, respectful relationship. Good mentors are willing:
- to serve as role models
- to give the time needed to develop the relationship
- to praise and disagree whenever necessary and appropriate
- to let go when the time comes, but still be available

Guidelines for Mentors

- Be dependable and on time. Your mentee is looking forward to seeing you. If you are unable to attend your scheduled meeting, you must notify the mentee as soon as possible. It is essential to maintain consistent attendance and regular participation.
- Work within the rules, policies and guidelines of the sponsoring organization, agency or institution.
- Greet your mentee with a smile and a positive attitude.
- Focus on being sensitive, fair, respectful and keep an open mind.

- Be patient, be prepared to call on your inner strength and peace before starting with a mentee. You will be tested for sincerity and commitment as soon as you are believed to be real.
- Learn about the mentee, i.e. nicknames, hobbies, favorites, etc. in order to develop a basis for a trusting relationship. The mentee's life story and the mentor's life story are important in the development of a successful mentor relationship.
- Ask them, "If you could be or do anything in the world, what would you be or what would you like to do?" Learn about the mentees goals and desires.
- Usually, the short term goals are undefined and the long term goals are almost always missing. Start off developing simple, achievable short term goals and work towards developing longer term goals.
- Help the mentee learn how to find and use local resources, such as the library, county extension, training and job opportunities, etc. Just pointing people in the right direction for getting answers to their questions or to see what is available is a tremendous help.
- Help the mentee see that his/her status is unique in the world though maybe not in his/her neighborhood and help him/her feel special about it, not inferior or unwanted. Teach him/her to see that people who speak or treat them badly are just mean people.
- Acknowledge a good job and even a good effort when you believe the mentee tried his/her best. Use partial success as a celebrative effort and help the mentee learn how to do even better the next time.

CREATIVITY AND MENTORING

- Concrete rewards like games, fruit, candy, pizza, or material gifts are often important symbols of caring. Over time these items should become less important and the genuine affection of the relationship should gradually replace the concrete rewards.
- In the case of puzzling behavior or responses, sensitively explore what else is going on in his/her world. Chances are good that something is wrong at home, at school, on the job or among friends.
- If the mentee's life experience has been filled with disappointment, don't expect trust to develop in a short time frame. Rule of thumb: For every year of life in a fractured, low income lifestyle expect at least a month of twice per week contact before there is genuine trust in the relationship.
- Roles and expectation should be clearly and sensitively defined, but not constraining. Patience and guidance are as important as structure and discipline.
- Allow yourself (mentor) to make mistakes, to be human and to forgive yourself. Use your failures, mistakes and frustrations for discussion with your mentee.
- Be empathetic towards the mentee. Communicate any concerns or problems with each other. If a compromise or agreement cannot be settled upon, relay the concerns or problems to the appropriate contact person or program sponsor.
- Make promises sparingly and keep them faithfully.
- Do not propose any religious doctrine, belief or alternate lifestyle to the mentee.

- Do not discuss your mentee and his/her problem(s) publicly or in social settings.

Successful Mentor Relationships

One day I decided to get my bicycle fixed and start riding for exercise. I took my bike to a gentleman who had worked on my bikes when I was a kid. Well, he had passed on and his widow wanted me to buy his tools and inventory. I happened to be between jobs and working on my masters thesis, plus she made me an offer I couldn't refuse. With the help of my Grandmother, I purchased it. We found an old garage near the local university campus and talked the landlord into letting us clean it out and use it for a bicycle shop.

I had enjoyed working on bicycles most of my childhood. So I got a comprehensive bicycle repair manual and began reading and gaining on the job experience. The woman who sold me the shop, said there was a man in town who might mentor me. This man just happened to be one of the sanitation workers that worked the neighborhood where the bicycle shop had relocated. I met him one day while he was picking up my trash and asked him if he would teach me about bicycles. He said yes and our mentoring relationship began.

We were an unlikely pair, me, a 30 year old, white collar Caucasian and James, a 50 year old, blue collar, African American. James had Wednesdays off, so I would take him the bicycles with problems I couldn't fix. He would teach me by showing me how to fix it. He had 22 years of experience with repairing bicycles which he graciously shared with me. We had a successful mentoring relationship which ended when we put the shop in storage and moved.

Maintaining a positive, optimistic, respectful attitude in a mentoring relationship is of paramount importance. It requires a real commitment of time and energy by the mentor and the mentee to create a successful mentor relationship. The most successful mentor relationships are entirely voluntary.

Approachability of the mentor is another important factor to a successful relationship. The mentee must feel comfortable enough in the relationship to ask questions, to be honest, and to share problems as they arise. There must be a climate of honesty and mutual respect as well as two-way communication in order for a mentor relationship to thrive.

The mentor plays many roles in the life of the mentee. One of the most powerful roles is that of model. The mentor must "practice what s/he preaches." Mentors must be living examples of how they wish their mentees to be and act. Mentors are teachers who provide mentees with a gold mine of practical knowledge, sharing wisdom gained through life and work experiences. At its best, mentoring is a one-on-one learning experience for both parties.

A mentor is a counselor who provides support, guidance, understanding and encouragement. The mentor possesses interpersonal knowledge and skills as well as technical knowledge and skills. Lea and Leibowitz (1983) identified ten roles that are usually performed by a mentor to benefit a mentee:
 1) teaching
 2) guiding
 3) advising
 4) counseling
 5) sponsoring

6) role modeling
7) validating
8) motivating
9) protecting
10) communicating

Mentoring is a two-way exchange and mentors also benefit from the relationship. According to Hall and Wessel (1987), the biggest reward is knowing that his/her hard-earned expertise will benefit the mentee. Successful mentor relationships are mutually beneficial, create opportunities and enhance learning which probably would not have occurred otherwise. The success of a mentor relationship depends upon mutual growth and contributions to each other's growth.

Family Mentorships

Mentor relationships exist in an endless variety of settings, circumstances, combinations, and personnel. The earliest mentor for a child is usually a close family member. Parents and other family members are particularly effective in assisting children and young people in the development of their creative strengths and potentials. In many rural areas, parents and family members are thrust into the mentor roles due to lack of resources and/or experts.

This was the case for Abigail Adams, mother of John Quincy Adams, the sixth President of the United States. Their town had lost its only school teacher, so Abigail became her son's teacher. She taught John to read and write. His learning was further stimulated by watching his mother single-handedly run their estate during the difficult times leading up to and through the American Revolution. Abigail's mentoring style combined firmness with kindness.

An essential function of the parental or familial mentor is to build the youth's self-esteem and provide support. Thomas Edison was labeled addled after three months of schooling when he was seven years old. His mother resented and rejected this evaluation. She decided to keep him at home and teach him herself. She sensed that the best approach was to let him follow his own interests. She led him through various subjects until she introduced him to science. At that point, his mind ignited and he started teaching himself. Later Edison said that his mother was his inspiration and strength. She understood him and let him explore and experience learning on his own.

Fathers as well as mothers can be powerful mentors for children and youth. One creative woman, in Torrance's 22-year longitudinal study (1980), called her father her most important mentor and wrote that he taught her the value of honesty. He was her friend who listened and encouraged her to try whatever she liked. He never condemned or berated her.

The parent-as-mentor role offers parents the opportunities to grow creatively with their children and to keep in touch with what their children are doing. Important bonding between children/youth and familial mentors can produce strength, courage and love for both individuals.

Gender Differences in Mentoring

Learning is a primary reason for the formation of mentoring relationships. In order to solve a new problem and/or gain new skills and knowledge, the mentee seeks help from an experienced person or expert.

Historically, most mentors have been men, partly because there are more men in positions to assume mentor roles. As more women move into executive positions and other leadership roles, there will be more women available to become mentors.

Women with male mentors reported a greater need for a more personal or friendship relationship than did their counterparts with female mentors (Torrance, 1984). Males more frequently prized their mentor's skill and expertise while females more frequently prized their mentor's encouragement and praise.

Males indicated that they need mentors who are: active, challenging, committed and dedicated, controversial, courageous, guiding, hardworking, involved, in love with his/her work, motivated for excellence, problem solvers, receptive and stern (Torrance, 1984, p. 12).

The characteristics of mentors which females indicated they need are: the ability to acknowledge talents of others, articulateness, calmness, considerate of alternatives, confidence giving, controlled, empathetic, enthusiastic, facilitative, even-tempered, humble, idealistic, patient, non-violent in philosophy, relaxed, thorough, vital and witty (Torrance, 1984, p. 12).

The characteristics which seemed to alienate women include: ambitiousness, compulsivity to work, critical in judgment, dominating and intimidating manner, lack of empathy, lack of future orientation, hypocrisy, intolerance of the ideas of others, inflexibility, perfectionism and trendiness (Torrance, 1984, p. 12).

Mentor Programs

Those who organize and foster mentor programs should recognize that the mentor in a relationship may in time become a friend, teacher, competitor, lover, or father/mother figure. If the relationship is a deep and caring one, any of these relationships may evolve. Fortunately, because of the caring nature of the mentor-mentee relationship, the outcomes are not likely to be harmful. Attention should be directed to the possible use of mentors for young children, especially disadvantaged or children at risk of not completing school.

Businesses, industries, schools and communities need to expand the pool from which they recruit mentors. While there is a need for the mentor with an eye for the future, there is also a need for the one with an historical orientation. Future oriented young people serving as mentors may lack some of the power and prestige of the usual pool of mentors. However, mentors influence the image each mentee has of the future and it would be foolhardy not to recognize and develop this group of potential mentors.

Retired persons in communities, grandparents and families provide another pool of possible mentors. Ehrlich (1983) urges parents to utilize the specialized knowledge of grandparents as mentors for children and youth. She maintains that grandparents will exert enormous energy locating special information to share with children.

Summary

I cannot stress the value of mentoring enough. Mentors come in all types, sizes and ages. Everyone is or has been a mentor to someone even though you may or may not know it. For some of us, mentoring is the way we learn best. We learn by doing and being guided by someone who knows what he/she is doing.

We (Torrance, Goff & Satterfield, 1998) have recently published a mentoring book for working with economically disasvantaged youth. It is entitled *Multicultural mentoring of the gifted and talented* by Prufrock Press. (For more information call - 800.998.2208, fax - 800.240.0333, Internet - www.prufrock.com)

Chapter 11
LIFELONG CREATIVITY

A young child fearlessly blurts out whatever thought comes to mind, with no evident censorship. Fairly soon, however, the child learns "the facts" as adults see them. Whenever s/he has a new idea or sees a new way of looking at something, the youngster is reminded of the "correct" view by the parent, teachers, employers, or other authority figures. By the time the youngster reaches adulthood, s/he is usually well conditioned to look only to authorities for any thoughts or ideas of worth. Thus, the work role becomes the preferred source of identity for most adults.

Our dependence on a work role as the source of identity is causing retirement to be a crisis. The crisis is finding meaning in life without being engaged in paid employment. At this point in life, leisure will either become an opportunity for growth and change or become a burden. Retirement often offers us the opportunity for self-development and understanding. The discovery or rediscovery of our creative talents and abilities leads to a positive attitude and peaceful state of mind. A program of self-development that intermingles leisure and creativity can immediately improve one's satisfaction with life.

Aging and Creativity

The proportion of people in the upper end of the life cycle is steadily and dramatically increasing. Increased life expectancies combined with early retirement makes todays' seniors the first adult group that must exist without having their life anchored in paid employment. A recurring problem with retirement is finding new meaning in life beyond the job.

Retirement can represent a separation not only from the job, but from friends, accustomed life patterns, accustomed physical environments, the very factors that give meaning and identity to life. Nonwork activities were often met with feelings of guilt over being nonproductive and lacking a role with which to identify. Retirement often results in large amounts of time to fill.

Leisure, therefore, is no longer a luxury but an essential of life (Neulinger, 1981). We must view nonwork as an opportunity for personal growth and/or development. Retirement provides opportunities for growth, learning, enrichment and the chance to build a better world. Leisure must be embraced with a positive attitude or it will become a burden.

Planning for the transition from the valued role of worker into the role-free life of retiree is often neglected or resisted. Retirement may lead to a decrease in satisfaction and meaningfulness of life. Life satisfaction is a state of mind where one is at peace with oneself and what one is doing (Neulinger, 1981).

In one study, I (Goff, 1993) examined the link between life satisfaction and creativity in older adults. A more detailed description of the study comes later in the chapter. The study appeared to empirically verify that a positive relationship does exist between creativity and life satisfaction. It verifies the hypothesis of Alpaugh, Renner and Birren (1976), that educational activities involving older adults in creative thinking can increase their life satisfaction as well as their creativity.

Retirement provides an optimal time for developing the creative abilities, strengths and talents in order to maintain or increase life satisfaction. Creative thinking is a lifestyle, a way of perceiving the world, a way of interacting with others. Living creatively is developing our talents, tapping our unused potential and becoming all that we are capable of becoming. Being creative is exploring new places, new ideas and taking risks. Being creative is developing a sensitivity to problems of nature and humankind.

Creativity is an ability often submerged or lying dormant in many adults. However, that creative spark remains alive and can be activated at any time. Creativity is facilitated by a healthy sense of change. Change is like a mobile. Change one part and the mobile is out of balance which only means that the old balance has been disturbed and there is new balancing to do.

Most often people either fear change or look forward to change. Those who fear change have the future image of something bad, of negative outcomes, of bad things happening and are paralyzed by their fear. People who look forward to change have the future image of something better, of positive outcomes, of good things happening and are energized by the possibilities. So much of how we feel and behave depends upon our point of view. If we change the way we look at things and the way we act, the outcomes will be different. Creative people look forward to change, to new possibilities, to the thrill of adventure and to what the unknown brings.

The community often provides a wide variety of opportunities for seniors. Many public insitutions can use the assistance of volunteers and sometimes part-time workers. Most local parks and recreation departments provide adult craft and hobby classes for small fees. I'm taking pottery right now at the community arts center and love it!

There are numerous organizations that organize leisure and educational trips and excursions for seniors. Elderhostel is a worldwide learning organization with locations all over the world. Elderhostel provides week long academic programs for seniors in college and university settings. For information contact Elderhostel, 75 Federal St., Boston, MA 02110.

Local senior centers often provide limited programming for seniors and are usually receptive to offering more activities and programs if someone wants to do it. Retirement centers and religious organizations often sponsor trips or activities for seniors.

The Internet is a growing resource for seniors and will require computer literacy. There are local services who teach beginning courses on using computers as well as vocational and technical schools who offer beginning and more advanced computer courses. You're never too old!

Creativity of Older Adults

In general, decrements in creativity have been associated with aging (Dohr & Forbess, 1986). However, studies have shown that creative attitudes and interests do not necessarily decline with age (Engleman, 1981) and even appear to change with intervening programs (Romaniuk, 1978). Dohr and Forbess (1986) found that older adults who participated in creative programs or who were creatively productive perceived an increase in creativeness with age, not decline.

In order to investigate the creativity of older adults, the Georgia Studies of Creative Behavior volunteered to conduct the creativity research section of a federally funded project, at the University of Georgia, aimed at integrating elderly individuals with developmental disabilities into their local senior centers. The Quality of Life Program was created to increase the independence of older adults (with and without developmental disabilities) and to integrate them into the community through physical and expressive activities designed to improve fitness, creativity and quality of life (Torrance, Clements & Goff, 1989).

The Quality of Life (QOL) Program involved five disciplines: art, creativity, dance, drama and fitness. Training modules developed for each of the five areas contained activities that incorporated physical, social, emotional and creative aspects of learning. The development of truly interdisciplinary, innovative, active and creative curriculum was a challenge. To meet this challenge, Torrance's Incubation Model of Teaching was used as the framework for every activity (Torrance & Safter, 1990). Teams of mentors and students from the five disciplines met regularly to brainstorm and integrate activities from the other disciplines into their own. The development of activities focused on play and fun which also contributed to the interdisciplinary nature of the activities.

The QOL activities recognized the creative spirit of the individuals as a central element of the life force and a key ingredient in healthful aging. Aging requires all of us to face situations which we have never encountered before. Some creativity is necessary whenever we face and address these new situations. When people of all ages are given practice in expression, their creativity improves (Torrance, 1987).

The QOL study involved 108 adults ages 51 years and older who were regular participants in 13 rural senior centers in Georgia. The experimental group, which consisted of 55 participants in 7 senior centers, received the QOL program three times per week for one hour over a period of four months. The control group consisted of 53 participants in 6 senior centers. These individuals were pre and post tested at the same time as the experimental group participants, but received no regularly scheduled educational activities during the four month interval between tests.

The results of the study indicated that the overall creativity, fluency and flexibility scores of the older adults who participated in the QOL Program increased significantly and may be attributed to the innovative, educational intervention (Goff, 1992). The increase in scores of the experimental group seems to support a growth theory for lifelong creativity. It appears that the QOL study results provide empirical evidence that older adults not only perceive an increase in their creativity but can actually increase their scores when they exercise their creative skills (Goff, 1992). Creativity can undergo a resurgence in the later years of life (Simonton, 1990).

A program of activities designed to enhance the creativity of older adults does provide opportunities for growth, self-expression, gaining a better understanding of self and others, and utilization of innate creative potential or self-actualization. Creative activities require a response from the inner self, one of the most important factors of well-being and enhanced mental health. According to Simonton (1990), the self-actualization process that motivates creativity will frequently drive an individual to surmount even the most debilitating infirmities of old age.

Self-expression and communication with oneself and others are essential for the growth of human beings, regardless of age. Creativity is a lifelong process which can be stimulated and enhanced at any age. Creative thinking skills are key elements of successful personal adjustments as well as meeting new challenges and dilemmas.

Brainstorming is a technique used throughout all three stages of the incubation model. This technique strengthens the imagination, flexible thinking and creativity. Brainstorming is one of the more teachable procedures for deliberately increasing the number (fluency), originality and quality of alternative ideas.

Senior Savvy Brainstormers Game

Brainstorming is an integral part of creative thinking and problem solving. It was felt that this skill would be extremely valuable to older adults to practice generating possible solutions and ideas in a fun atmosphere. Thus grew the idea of Senior Savvy Brainstormers, a board game for older adults. It was created to teach groups of people how to brainstorm.

Group brainstorming sessions are very important because people spark each other's imagination. Little ideas can lead to bigger ones or answers to questions.

Group brainstorming helps stretch their ideas and exercise their minds. The game is also a great socializer. People of all ages and all walks of life are successful at playing the game, especially in groups.

In brainstorming, all answers and ideas are correct, thus removing the threat of not knowing the right answer. The only pressure on each player is to contribute just one idea or answer in a 60 second period. We have played Senior Savvy Brainstormers with all types and sizes of groups of older adults, intergenerational groups and families with great success. The game inspires laughter and a good time. Brainstorming keeps the mind active and alert. It's mental exercise which is essential for vibrant, aging adults. (For information about Senior Savvy Brainstormers call 405-372-0810 or fax 405-377-5284 or e-mail: mcgoff@cowboy.net).

Summary

As a person grows psychologically and copes with his/her constantly changing environment and self, creativity is called into play. Using our creativity, increases our creativity. So by using our creativity, we develop our creativity and become more self-actualized. We become more fully-functioning, healthier, use more of our talents and gain a better understanding of who we are and what we contribute to ourselves and those around us.

As we age we gain a wealth of experience, knowledge, skills and wisdom which are many of the qualities necessary for creativity (Clark & Osgood, 1985). The creative potential and self-actualization of older adults have virtually been ignored. Older adults represent a steadily increasing reservoir of untapped resources. We can no longer afford to ignore the potential contribution to society from this segment of the population.

Hey I've been there.
Take a shortcut
& bypass the
red tape...
Network!
Collaborate!
Try this....

Chapter 12
CREATIVITY TIPS

As you continue on your journey into the world of creativity, a couple of tips may prove helpful. I use these tips in my daily life and hope they will assist you in exploring your creativity and the creativity of others.

Tips for Increasing Your Creativity

- Look for the second right answer. Often the really creative idea is just around the corner.
- The answers you get depend on the questions you ask. Play with your wording and get different answers.
- Challenge the rules you use to govern your day-to-day activities.
- Cultivate your imagination. Set aside time everyday to ask yourself "what if" questions.
- Strengthen your "risk muscle." Being creative requires risk taking.
- Be flexible. Open yourself to experiences, do something you have always wanted to do.
- Failure only means you know what does not work and gives you the opportunity to try a new approach.

- Let the kid inside of you out. Let your "stupid" monitor down and have some fun. See how many crazy ideas you can come up with.

Look for the second right answer. Often the really creative idea is just around the corner. Once you get past the idea of one right answer, we next become comfortable with three, such as:
- yes, no, maybe
- go, yield, stop
- on your mark, get set, go
- green, yellow, red
- beginning, middle, end

The first thing to do is to train yourself to delay judgment and to think of three possible answers/solutions instead of the single right answer. For example:

1 plus 1 equals 2
1 and 1 are eleven
1 bubble plus 1 bubble equals 1 bubble

By using your imagination you can break the stereotype and become creative. How many different solutions can you come up with to questions or problems you thought only had one right answer? You might want to write them down along with as many different solutions as you can think of.

Once you are comfortable with stretching yourself to three possibilities, try four. Many times getting the fourth answer/solution opens the doors to truly creative possibilities. Once we break past the comfort of three, stretching to four leads to five and six, where the really creative, productive answer or solution can be found. Usually when dealing with questions/problems we use what is familiar to answer/address them, sometimes using what is comfortable and familiar instead of using what is best and may require change.

Many times we fear change more than we fear repeating the same mistakes. Fear of change is the result of our negative expectations of the change. Many times we are motivated toward change because it just couldn't be any worse. However, if the motivation for change is looked at as a positive, then things will be even better than they are now. Change presents new challenges and experiences from which we grow.

The answers you get depend on the question you ask. Children are excellent questioners. They ask very real questions that adults often times dismiss. Every time an adult dismisses a child's question, the child learns not to ask questions, that asking good questions is not a good, rewarded thing to do. So at a very early age, we begin to lose our ability to ask good questions, especially if we are considered "trouble makers" for asking questions which we would truly like answered. Therefore many of the communications problems we encounter as adults are due to our inability to ask good questions - we just haven't had much practice. Play with your wording to get different answers.

- Do we have to go downtown?
- Wouldn't you love to go downtown?
- Let's go downtown, ok?
- Aren't you going downtown with me?
- Must we go downtown?

- Wouldn't you like to take me downtown?
- I'll buy lunch if you will go downtown with me, what do you say?

Body language, tone of voice, facial expressions, and emotions also influence the answers to questions. My mother volunteered to participate in a geriatric research project at the local university. As part of her screening, she was administered several standardized tests. One question in particular asked how much she agreed to the statement - "Big people intimidate me." Well, she said, "it depends if they are trying to intimidate me or not, but there was no place for that answer." One question on the depression scale asked if she looked forward to getting up in the morning. My mother is not a morning person, and said no, but that once she's up she looks forward to her day. So by answering that she doesn't look forward to getting up in the morning does that mean she's depressed? You can see that sometimes the answers you get depend upon the questions you ask.

Challenge the rules you use to govern your day-to-day activities. Many times we fall into habits, ruts and routines that are not the best use of our time and energy. We may even be aware that there are better ways, but are too comfortable with "our way" to change or alter our routine. Our minds become lazy and out of shape as we fall under the seduction of repetition and ruts. We mindlessly follow set patterns and rules without noticing what is going on around us.

For example, the morning ritual is timed to the minute by most of us. We know what time we need and the steps necessary to get up and out to work or school on time. The thought of changing or even thinking about changing our morning routine makes most of us shiver. It would either make us late or we would forget an important step in the process if we alter it - is what most of us think. However, what if changing the routine would give us more time, rather than less time to complete our steps. By changing my routine and picking out what I was going to wear the next day, the night before, I have saved valuable time and frustration.

Observe how you do things and try doing them differently. Take a different route to work. Play the role of some famous person for a day. Have you ever noticed how people at work react when you act differently than usual, such as being quiet when you usually are not, or late when you are usually on time, etc. People get comfortable with things as they are and notice when things are not as they usually are.

When I was teaching high school, I taught Spanish the first two hours and Current Events the third hour. As an experiment, I rearranged the seating arrangement in the room every day. They never knew how the room would be set up. I didn't really know if it was having any kind of effect until the Spanish classes had an exam. On that day I didn't rearrange the chairs and left them in straight rows. When the Current Events class came in they threw a fit, because the chairs were in straight rows. "You can't do this", they cried. "I can't do what?", I said. "You can't put the chairs in rows like everybody else." It was then I knew that my experiment was effective.

Cultivate your imagination. Set aside time everyday to ask yourself "what if" questions. What if Ed McMahon did come to your door with a million dollar prize, what would you do? Many times we get so emersed in the responsibilities and obligations of life that we forget to dream or play with ideas and possibilities. We are very familiar with using our imaginations for worry and anxiety, but many times we are less familiar with out hopes and dreams.

In our search for answers/solutions, we often take what is quick rather than devoting the necessary time to thinking of a really good solution. Our insatiable appetite for quick and easy fixes, rarely permits us time to think or to use our imaginations to discover a better solution or answer. Creative thinking takes time for one thing to lead to another and requires the use of the imagination.

Often the fuel for my imagination is nature. Being out in the wilderness and experiencing it with all of my senses revitalizes and rejuvenates me. The smells, the sounds, the sights, the different textures, all a beautiful panorama of wonder and awe. Many inventions are adaptations of nature and many great works of art are reflections of nature. Nature provides a free show all day everyday - sunrises, sunsets, full moons, stars, plants, animals . . . . By observing and experiencing nature, you create sensory images which can be recalled and used to cultivate the imagination.

Strengthen your "risk muscle." Make it a point to take at least one risk every 24 hours. This doesn't mean to go sky diving or bungee jumping everyday unless you would like to do these things. It means doing some little something differently than you usually do. For example, if you are a punctual person, be late to a meeting and watch the reaction. Or if you are a tardy person, be on time for once and see what people say or how they acknowledge your change. If you are the silent type, make some noise sometime and see how people react. If you are the extrovert, consciously be quiet for a day and see how many people ask if you're feeling or doing OK. "Taking risks" means experimenting with life, gaining experiences and learning about yourself and others.

I have taken a couple of risks by auditioning for summer musicals put on by the local community theater. I have played townspeople and had a ball. Also, I have met some really fine people and would recommend this risk to anyone who has moved to a new town and is having trouble meeting creative people.

By strengthening your risk muscle, you are increasing your courage and usually self-confidence. By trying something you haven't tried before you are being courageous. Trying something and being able to say you tried it, is both satisfying and gratifying.

Having a positive future image of what is going to result from taking the risk, makes the risk easier to take. Believing that I was going to get chosen to be in the musicals, made it easier for me to go try out. I'm sure it also contributed to a more confident audition.

Be flexible. Open yourself to experiences, do something you have always wanted to do. You work hard and deserve enjoyment in your life. The only way to make a dream come true is to go about achieving or experiencing it. That means action - schedule time away, make an appointment to do something, sign up to take a class, visit a museum or gallery - do something good for yourself that is pure, innocent fun.

In order to embrace change, you must be flexible and defer judgment. For example, if you didn't like cooked carrots when you were little, don't assume your tastes have not changed as you have matured. Be flexible, try them again, maybe with a little butter and pinch of brown sugar on them. Being flexible can mean examining and testing what we learned as kids to see if those same lessons apply now that we are adults. The more different experiences we have, the more flexible we will be. That's why diversity is a strength, not a weakness.

Failure only means that we know what does not work and gives us the opportunity to try a new approach or practice to get better. More often than not, we take "failure" to mean we are inadequate or incompetent because we didn't get it right or do it well the first time. Many times we deceive ourselves into believing that if it looks easy, then it must be and, of course, anyone can do it. We fail to take into account that the reason it looks so effortless or easy is because it is being performed by a professional or expert with years of practice and performance experience. It is really pretty ridiculous to think that the first time we do something that we will be competent and as successful as a seasoned veteran. Awareness and acceptance of the role of novice or beginner makes it easier to be creative and try new things.

I took a cake decorating class once. I love color and thought it would be a blast making beautiful, edible art. The instructor was a forty year veteran and created beautiful decorations and made it look so easy. I was plugging along fairly well, a little frustrated, but OK until we came to roses. Needless to say the rose she made so effortlessly looked like globby clumps of discs when I made them. I was exasperated and was experiencing stress. My relaxing leisure activity had now turned into a stressful set of obstacles. The

CREATIVITY TIPS

teacher suggested that some of us might need to go to "happy hour" before next week's class so we'd be more relaxed.

After that class, I began to analyze the situation. Why was it so stressful? Because my roses weren't perfect. Why did my roses need to be perfect since I was just a beginner? No one's roses were perfect, why did I think mine needed to be? How was I going to make the class fun instead of stressful?

I realized that it was pretty silly to think I could decorate a cake as well as a seasoned veteran. I began to realize that I learn best through trial and error rather than through perfection. The next class, without going to happy hour, I relaxed and found that I learned more from my mistakes (practice) than from the instructions. So I began to laugh at my unique creations and "learning by doing" style. It didn't take long for my classmates to also learn from my unique interpretations of the instructions. I think we learned more from my "failures" than we did from the instructor's perfection.

Let the kid inside of you out and play. Let your "stupid monitor" down and have some fun. See how many "crazy" ideas you can come up with. Put on a Halloween mask and drive around town. Borrow a friends' car, if you live in a small town, so they get the credit for wearing the mask. This is especially effective when it's not Halloween.

When someone cuts you off in traffic, or pulls out in front of you and goes slow, smile and wave at them instead of cursing and flipping them off. I have had the most fun being nice to people when they think I'm going to be ugly. We tend to be ugly when we get behind the wheel of a moving vehicle. I think if we would sing more; watch the clocks less; listen to music; read books and experience the arts, that we would all be more playful.

Play is an important ingredient in a healthy life. Being spontaneous and playful keeps us young and gives us zest for life. Healthy play combined with hard work leads to a successful life. Whether life is seen as an opportunity or a burden depends on one's point of view, not one's circumstances.

We often forget to include ourselves when we are being good to others. We have learned not to be selfish which we translate to mean we are not supposed to be good to ourselves. However, only when we feel good about ourselves and treat ourselves with the same goodness and respect we give others, are we truly happy and healthy. Being kind to ourselves lets us be kinder to others.

One way to check on ourselves is to examine our self-talk or inner dialogue. If you would not say to another person the things you say to yourself, then do not say them to yourself either. Negative self-talk and self-criticism keep us from being creative, positive contributors to our students, friends, families and communities.

Summary

Creativity is the gift that keeps on giving, to ourselves and others, for as long as we want. It takes place in the minds of all of us. Creativity is an internal, self-motivating life force that generates and sustains its own energy. It is a natural process.

APPENDIX A

Ideas for Activities

Here are some activities I have used with children and adults to enhance their creativity:

1.) Put the individualls into small groups of 4-5 students per group. Provide them with a 3-4 feet length and 3-4 feet width butcher paper banner and something to paint, mark or color or decorate it with. Ask each group to illustrate what they think play looks like. I usually allow 20-30 minutes for groups to illustrate a topic I give them. Other topics which might be used include: love, peace, friendship, happiness, freedom, laughter, harmony....

Following completion of the banners, each groups is asked to describe their banner and are then assisted in hanging them on the wall or some other appropriate place for them to be displayed. This activity teaches that even when asked to do the same thing, the banners are all unique and original. Be sure to point out how they are all different and wonderfully creative!

2.) People love games and having them work together and invent a game is exciting and rewarding. The ages of the participants will determine how simple this activity needs to be and how much preparation you will need to do. The younger the person, the more preparatory planning there needs to be. Older children can take some of the responsibility for their learning - like bringing items from home.

Again put the participants into groups of 4-5 and ask them to create a game. The supplies they begin with will be determined and provided by you with consideration of their ages. Older children can be asked to identify the parts they will need and assisted

APPENDIX A

in obtaining or making them. Children love this activity and will usually spend as much time on their games as you allow. Their finished products are shared with each other and they are all given the opportunity to play each other's games.

3.) Children love to play with clay. Very young children learn by manipulating, experimenting and exploring and clay lends itself to these learning skills. Clay is fairly inexpensive and can be purchased in 25 pound boxes at hobby stores, ceramic stores or pottery supply stores. If you purchase clay in bulk, be sure to use fishing line to cut it up. If you do not have access to clay or would rather make you own, here's a recipe.

Scented Play Dough

2 c. flour
2 c. cold water
1/3 c. salt
2 Tbs. cream of tartar
2 Tbs. + 1 tsp. oil
2-3 pkgs. of flavored gelatin
    red - cherry, strawberry
    green - lime
    blue - berries
    purple - grape
    orange - orange

- Put all ingredients into blender or food processor
- Mix until smooth
- Cook in heavy sauce pan low heat 'til thick (like mashed potatoes)
- Stir constantly!
- Let cool completely

Provide each child with clay or play dough. Ask each child to make a favorite toy or something they love. Allow 20-30 minutes for them to manipulate and play with the clay. When they have all finished ask each child to share his/her sculpture and tell a little about it. This activity gives children an opportunity to explore and express themselves using their sense of touch.

4.) People of all ages love to play with colors by painting to music. Wall painting is an exciting activity. Cover a wall with good quality butcher paper and the floor with a drop cloth. Have a variety of styles and types of music to play as participants paint on the wall - the longer the wall, the better. After the participants have had an opportunity to paint, ask each one to share what it felt like and how did they feel when the music was changed.

This activity might translate into a community project in which a local citizen might allow the participants to paint the exterior wall of a barn, business, garage or storage shed. This could be orchestrated with the help of other community members. Try to get the paint and supplies donated. Be creative!

Appendix B

Sample Incubation Model of Teaching Lesson
Developing the Imagination
"A Peaceful Place"

Supplies:
- colored markers
- paper

I. **Warm-up**

Just for a moment I want all of you to take a deep breath and relax. Again, breathe in, hold it and exhale. This time I want you to breathe in, take all of your thoughts and put them into that breath and blow them out as you exhale. Clear you mind of all thoughts, cares and worries. Ready, breathe in, gather your thoughts and now blow them out with the air. Exhale.

Now, please get in a comfortable position. Most people can concentrate better with their eyes closed, but this is optional. We are going to take a short mental journey. I want you to take yourself to your favorite place for relaxation - the beach, the mountains, a meadow, Paris, your backyard - wherever you feel happy, relaxed and at peace.

Listen to the sounds, what do you hear? Waves? Running water? Birds? Music? Quiet? What do you hear?

What do you see? Blue sky? Palm trees? Mountain tops? Billowy clouds? What do you see?

What do you smell? Salt water? Crisp, fresh air? Flowers? Fresh bread? What do you smell?

What tastes are you experiencing? Sweetness? Saltiness? Sourness? Bitterness? What do you taste?

What textures are in your peaceful place? Roughness? Smoothness? Grittiness? Softness? What can you touch and feel?

How do you feel? Safe? Happy? Secure? Relaxed? Excited? How do you feel?

Pay very close attention to all of your senses while you are enjoying your peaceful hideaway. When I count to 3, I want you to return to this room. Ready, 1..., 2..., 3..., open your eyes and you are back. You should feel relaxed and refreshed.

II. Dig-in

Now, I want you to use the markers to illustrate your peaceful hideaway on the paper provided. The focus is not on your artistic ability, but on your ability to put your ideas on paper! Let's take 15 minutes to do this. Everyone will have the opportunity to describe your peaceful hideaway.

III. Go Beyond

We will go around the room and let each person describe his/her peaceful hideaway. After everyone has had a chance to discuss his/her illustration, lead a discussion of what they learned from the experience:
1. Everyone was read the same scenario, yet every illustration different. Why?
2. How difficult was it to imagine a peaceful hideaway using all of the senses? Which senses were easier or more difficult to imagine?
3. How difficult was it to translate your thoughts into an illustration? Was your imagined hideaway in color?

I want each of you to put your peaceful hideaway illustration somewhere where you can see it and to refer to it anytime you feel stressed or uptight.

Our culture has not valued the importance of everyday imagination and as a result, imagery is often equated with the fanciful, the unreal and the impractical. Some do not realize that they are using their imaginations when rehearsing a sales presentation, a job interview or an obstacle course. Worry and anxiety are powerful, stressful examples of our imaginations at work. Creating a new program, writing a proposal or solving problems are positive examples of our imaginations at work.

A common therapeutic use of mental imagery is the indication of a state of relaxation, like the activity above. Relaxation visualizations reverse the effects of stress. During the above activity, your heart rates slowed, blood pressure fell, muscle reactions were diminished, hormonal secretions changed, pain was diminished and each one of you experienced a lessening of worry and anxiety.

Mental images are not only effective motivational tools for recovering health, but also important tools for self-discovery, problem solving and making creative changes in other areas of our lives. Every time we meet a problem or dilemma for which we have no learned solution, some degree of creativity is required.

APPENDIX B

Sample of a Service Delivery Strategy for At-risk Students Using the Incubation Model of Teaching

I. Warm-up

Students who have been identified as being at-risk are presented with vocabulary words, background information and previous concepts necessary for learning the material, which will be presented to the whole class later, by a tutor or learning assistant. This will enhance the students' comprehension level when the material is presented in class.

II. Dig-in

All students are presented with the academic information which will appear on future quizzes or exams. This is the instructional segment in which students are presented with materials that they will be held accountable for learning.

III. Go Beyond

The tutor or learning assistant and the student work together to identify the key points of the material presented, review class notes and jointly develop a comprehensive test over the materials presented. The tutor or learning assistant presents the test to the classroom teacher who approves it or makes necessary changes. The tutor/learning assistant prepares the individualized test so that it looks as much like theclassroom exam as possible. On exam day, the at-risk student takes the exam at the same time and in the same setting as their classroom peers.

REFERENCES

The AAUW Report: How schools shortchange girls. (1995). New York: Marlowe & Company.

Achterberg, J. (1985). *Imagery in healing: Shamanism and modern medicine.* Boston: Shambhala.

Alpaugh, P. K., Renner, V. J., & Birren, J. E. (1976). Age and creativity: Implications for education and teachers. *Educational Gerontology, 1*, 27-40.

Amabile, T. M. (1989). *Growing up creative.* NY: Crown Publishers.

Anthony, R. (1984). *The ultimate secrets of total self confidence.* NY: Berkeley Books.

Arieti, S. (1976). *Creativity: The magic synthesis.* NY: Basic Books, Inc.

Barsky, M. (1985). The creative powers within us. In N. Weisberg & R. Wilder (Eds.), *Creative arts with older adults* (pp. 145-154). NY: Human Sciences Press, Inc.

Blatner, A. & Blatner, A. (1988). *The art of play.* NY: Human Sciences press.

Bogen, J. E. (1969). The other side of the brain II: An oppositional mind. *Bulletin of the Los Angeles Neurological Societies, 34*, 135-162.

Borysenko, J. (1988). *Minding the body, mending the mind.* NY: Bantam New Age Books.

Bowen, W. P. & Mitchell, E. D. (1925). *The theory of organized play.* NY: A. S. Barnes & Co.

Carter, R. T. (1990). Cultural differences in learning. *Journal of College Development, 31*(1), 71-79.

Clark, P. & Osgood, N. J. (1985). *Seniors on stage*. NY: Praeger Publishers.

Cornett, C. E. (1986). *Learning through laughter: Humor in the classroom*. Bloomington, IN: Phi Delta Kappa Educational Foundation.

Cropley, A. J. (1990). Creativity and mental health in everyday life. *Creativity Research Journal, 3*(3), 167-178.

Dacey, J. S. (1976). *New ways to learn: The psychology of education*. NY: A. S. Barnes & Co.

Dohr, J. H. & Forbess, L. A. (1986). Creativity, arts and profiles of aging: A reexamination. *Educational Gerontology, 12*, 123-138.

Dubois, P. (1907). *The influence of the mind on the body*. NY: Funk & Wagnalls Co.

Dunn, H. L. (1961). *High level wellness*. Arlington, VA: R. W. Beatty, Ltd.

Eberle, R. F. (1971). *SCAMPER: Games for imagination development*. Buffalo, NY: D.O.K.

Edwards, B. (1979). *Drawing on the right side of the brain*. LA: Jeremy P. Tarcher, Inc.

Engleman, M. (1981). The response of older women to a creative problem-solving program. *Educational Gerontology, 6*, 165-173.

Flack, J. D. (1989). *Inventing, inventions and inventors*. Englewood, CO: Teacher Ideas Press.

Fleshman, B. & Fryrear, J. L. (1981). *The arts in therapy*. Chicago: Nelson-Hall.

Fobes, R. (1993). *The creative problem solver's toolbox*. Corvallis, OR: Solutions Through Innovation.

Freud, S. (1910). *Three contributions of the theory of sex*. NY: Nervous and Mental Disease Publishing Co.

REFERENCES

Gardner, H. (1983). *Frame of mind: A theory of multiple intelligences.* NY: Basic Books, Inc.

Glasser, W. (1986). *Control theory in the classroom.* NY: Basic Books.

Goff, K. (1992). Enhancing creativity in older adults. *Journal of Creative Behavior, 26*(1), 40-49.

Goff, K. (1993). Creativity and life satisfaction of older adults. *Educational Gerontology, 19*, 241-250.

Goff, K. & Torrance, E. P. (Spring, 1991). The Georgia Studies of Creative Behavior: Venturing into studies of creativity of the elderly. *Generations*, 53-54.

Green, E. & Green, A. (1977). *Beyond biofeedback.* San Francisco: Delacorte Press.

Hall, V. M. & Wessel, J. A. (June 14, 1987). Wise counseling by a mentor can greatly enrich a career. *Atlanta Journal/Atlanta Constitution*, 57.

Helson, R. M. (1978). Creativity in women. In J. A. Sherman and F. L. Denmark (Eds.), *The psychology of women: Future directions in research* (p. 555-604). NY: Psychological Dimensions, Inc.

Hermann, N. (1987). *The creative brain.* Lake Lure, NC: Brain Dominance Institute.

Hill, D. J. (1988). *Humor in the classroom: A handbook for teachers (and other entertainers).* Springfield, IL: Charles C. Thomas.

Isaksen, S. G. & Treffinger, D. J. (1985). *Creative problem solving: The basic course.* Buffalo, NY: Bearly Limited.

Johnson, D. W. & Johnson, R. T. (1989). *Cooperation and competition: Theory and research.* Edina, MN: Interaction Books.

Kaplan, K. L. (1995). Women's voices in organizational development: Questions, stories and implications. *Journal of Organizational Change Management, 8*(1), 52-90.

Kauffman, D. L. (1976). *Teaching the future*. Palm Springs, CA: ETC Publications.

Keohane, N. O. (1990). Educating women students for the future. In J. Antler & S. K. Biklen (Eds.), *Changing education: Women as radicals and conservatives* (p. 3-12). NY: State University of New York Press.

Klein, A. (1989). *The healing power of humor*. Los Angeles: Jeremy P. Tarcher, Inc.

Koestler, A. (1964). *The act of creation*. London: Macmillan.

Korn, E. R. & Johnson, K. (1983). *Visualization: The uses of imagery in the health professions*. Homewood, IL: Dow Jones-Irwin.

Landrum, G. N. (1994). *Profiles of female genius*. NY: Prometheus Books.

Lea, D. & Leibowitz, Z. B. (April, 1983). A mentor: Would you know one if you saw one? *Supervising Management, 28*(4), 32-25.

Lowenfeld, V. & Brittain, W. (1970). *Creative and mental growth*. NY: Macmillan Co.

Macdonald, A. L. (1992). *Feminine ingenuity: Women and invention in America*. NY: Ballantine Books.

Maier, N. R. (1970). *Problem-solving and creativity in iindividuals and groups*. Belmont, CA: Brooks-Cole.

Marsiske, M. & Willis, S. L. (in press). Practical creativity in older adults everyday problem solving: Life-span perspectives. In C. E. Adams-Price (Ed.), *Creativity and aging: Theoretical and empirical approaches*. NY: Springer.

Maslow, A. H. (1959). Creativity and self-actualizing people. In H. H. Anderson (Ed.), *Creativity and its cultivation* (p. 83-95). NY: Harper & Brothers.

Maslow, A. (1962). *Toward a psychology of being*. NY: D. Van Nostrand.

REFERENCES

Maslow, A. H. (1962). Emotional blocks to creativity. In S. J. Parnes & H. F. Harding (Eds), *A source book for creative thinking* (pp. 93-103). NY: Charles Scribner's Sons.

Maslow, A. H. (1968). *Toward a psychology of being* (2nd ed.). Princeton, NJ: Van Nostrand.

Maslow, A. H. (1971). *The farther reaches of human nature.* NY: Viking Press.

Maslow, A. H. (1987). *Motivation and personality* (3rd. ed.). NY: HarperCollins Publishers.

Matte, N. L. & Henderson, S. H. G. (1995). *Success your style!* Belmont, CA: Wadsworth Publishing Co.

McCaslin, N. (1984). *Creative drama in the classroom* (4th ed.). NY: Longman.

McCracken, J. L. (1997). *Women who invent: Examining the impact of formal and informal education on their creativity.* Unpublished doctoral dissertation, Oklahoma State University.

McGhee, P. E. (1979). *Humor: Its origin and development.* San Francsico: W. H. Freeman and Co.

McNiff, S. (1986). *Educating the creative arts therapist.* Springfield, IL: Charles C. Thomas.

Millar, G. W. (1997). *E. Paul Torrance - "The Creativity Man": An authorized Biography.* Norwood, NJ: Ablex Publishing Co.

Moody, R. A. (1978). *Laugh after laugh: The healing power of humor.* Jacksonville, FL: Headwaters Press.

Moussa, F. (1991). *Women inventors.* Geneva: Farag Moussa.

Murdock, M. C. & Torrance, E. P. (1988). Using the Torrance sociodrama model as a vehicle for negotiation. *Creative Child and Adult Quarterly, 13*(3), 108-114.

Neulinger, J. (1981). *The psychology of leisure.* Springfield, IL: Charles C. Thomas.

Ornstein, R. & Sobel, D. (1987). *The healing brain*. NY: Simon & Schuster, Inc.

Osborn, A . F. (1953). *Applied imagination*. NY: Charles Scribners Sons.

Osborn, A. (1963). *Applied imagination* (3rd ed.). NY: Charles Scribner's.

Parnes, S. J. (1967). *Creative behavior guidebook*. NY: Charles Scribners Sons.

Parnes, S. J. (1992). Creative problem solving and visionizing. In S. J. Parnes & H. F. Harding (Eds.), *Sourcebook for creative problem solving* (p. 133-154). Buffalo, NY: Creative Education Foundation.

Parnes, S. J. (1997). *Optimize: The magic of your mind*. Buffalo, NY: Bearly Limited.

Pelletier, K. R. (1977). *Mind as healer, mind as slayer*. NY: Delta.

Philbin, M., Meier, E., Huffman, S. & Boverie, P. (1995). A survey of gender and learning styles. *Sex Roles, 32*(7/8), 485-494.

Phipho, C. (1992). Caught between competing visions. *Phi Delta Kappan, 74*(2), 102-103.

Piirto, J. (1991). Why are there so few? (Creative women: Visual artists, mathematicians, musicians). *Roeper Review, 13*(3), 142-147.

Pohlman, L. (1996). Creativity, gender and the family: A study of creative writers. *Journal of Creative Behavior, 30*(1), 1-24.

Putnam, J. W. (Ed). (1993). *Cooperative learning and strategies for inclusion: Celebrating diversity in the classroom*. Baltimore: Paul H. Brookes.

Resnick, L. (1990). Literacy in school and out. *Dedalus, 119*(2), 169-185.

REFERENCES

Restak, R. (1991). *The brain has a mind of its own.* NY: Crown Trade Paperbacks.

Robinson, V. M. (1991). *Humor and the health professions.* Thorofare, NJ: Slack.

Romaniuk, J. G. (1978). Training creativity in the elderly: An examination of attitudes, self-perception and abilities. (Doctoral dissertation, University of Wisconsin-Madison). *Dissertation Abstracts International, 39*, 2841A.

Rogers, C. R. (1962). Toward a theory of creativity. In S. J. Parnes & H. F. Harding (Eds.), *A source book for creative thinking* (pp. 66-72). NY: Scribner's.

Rossman, M. L. (1987). *Healing yourself.* NY: Walker & Co.

Scribner, S. (1986). Thinking in action: Some chacteristics of practical thought. In R. J. Sternberg & R. K. Wagner (Eds.), *Practical intelligence: Nature and origins of competence in the everyday world* (p. 13-30). NY: Cambridge University Press.

Selye, H. (1974). *Stress without distress.* NY: J. B. Lippincott Co.

Showell, E. H. & Amram, F. M. B. (1995). *From Indian corn to outer space women invent in America.* NY: Cobblestone Publishing.

Simonton, D. K. (1990). Creativity in the later years: Optimistic prospects for achievement. *Gerontologist, 30*, 626-631.

Simonton, O. C. & Matthews-Simonton, S. (1979). Stress, self-regulation and cancer. In E. M. Goldwag (Ed.), *Inner balance: The power of holistic healing* (pp. 122-138). Englewood Cliffs, NJ: Prentice-Hall, Inc.

Simonton, O. C. & Matthews-Simonton, S. (1984). A psychophysiological model of intervention in the treatment of cancer. In J. S. Gordon, D. T. Jaffe & D. E. Bresler (Eds.), *Mind, body and health* (pp. 146-163). NY: Vintage Books.

Sperry, R. W. (1968). Hemisphere disconnection and unity in conscious awareness. *American Psychologist, 23*, 723-733.

Taggart, W. & Torrance, E. P. (1984). *Human information processing survey.* Bensonville, IL: Scholastic Testing Service.

Taylor, K. & Marienau, C. (1995). Learning environments for women's adult development: Bridges toward change. *New Directions for Adult and Continuing Education, 65*, 1-3.

Torrance, E. P. (1957a). Psychology of survival. Unpublished manuscript, Air Force Personnel Research Center, Lackland Air Force Base, TX.

Torrance, E. P. (1957b). Group decision making and disagreement. *Social Forces, 35*, 314-318.

Torrance, E. P. (1962). *Guiding creative talent.* Englewood Cliffs, NY: Prentice-Hall.

Torrance, E. P. (1963). *Education and the creative potential.* Minneapolis, MN: University of Minnesota Press.

Torrance, E. P. (1965a). *Rewarding creative behavior.* Englewood Cliffs, NJ: Prentice-Hall

Torrance, E. P. (Fall, 1965b). Helping the creatively gifted girl achieve her potentiality. *Journal of National Association of Women Deans and Counselors*, 28-33.

Torrance, E. P. (1971). Creativity and infinity. *Journal of Research and Development in Education, 4*(3), 35-41.

Torrance, E. P. (1972a). Creative young women in today's world. *Exceptional Children*, 597-603.

REFERENCES

Torrance, E. P. (1972b). Creative kids. *Today's Education, 61*(1), 25-28.

Torrance, E. P. (1975a). Creative kids. In E. P. Torrance and W. F. White (Eds.), *Issues and advances in educational psychology* (p. 233-238). Istasca, IL: F. E. Peacock Publishers, Inc.

Torrance, E. P. (1975b). Sociodrama as a creative problem sovling approach to studying the future. *Journal of Creative Behavior, 9*, 182-195.

Torrance, E. P. (1976). Give the gifted children of the world a chance to solve future problems. *Talents and Gifts, 18*(3), 22-24.

Torrance, E. P. (1977a). *Creativity in the classroom.* Washington, DC: National Education Association.

Torrance, E. P. (1977b). *Discovery and nurturance of giftedness in the culturally different.* Reston, VA: Council for Exceptional Children.

Torrance, E. P. (1978a). Healing qualities of creative behavior. *Creative Child and Adult Quarterly, 3*, 146-168.

Torrance, E. P. (1978b). What happens when gifted children study the future. Paper presented at the TAG Midwest Regional Conference, Eastern Michigan University, Ypsilanti, MI, October 13, 1978.

Torrance, E. P. (1979). *The search for creativity and satori.* Buffalo, NY: Bearly Limited.

Torrance, E. P. (1980). Creativity and futurism in education: Retooling. *Education, 100*, 298-311.

Torrance, E. P. (1983). Role of mentors in creative achievement. *Creative Child and Adult Quarterly, 8*, 8-15, 18.

Torrance, E. P. (1984). *Mentor relationships.* Buffalo, NY: Bearly Limited.

Torrance, E. P. (1987). *Using the Torrance Tests of Creative Thinking to guide the teaching of creative behavior.* Bensenvilel, IL: Scholastic Testing Service, Inc.

Torrance, E. P. (1988). The nature of creativity as manifest in its testing. In R. G. Sternberg (Ed.), *The nature of creativity: Contemporary perspectives* (p. 43-75). NY: Cambridge University Press.

Torrance, E. P. (1992). Creatively gifted learning disabled individuals. *Educational Forum, 56*(4), 399-404.

Torrance, E. P. (1995a). *Why fly? A philosophy of creativity.* Norwood, NJ: Ablex Publishing Corp.

Torrance, E. P. (1995b). Insights about creativity: Questioned, rejected, ridiculed, ignored. *Educational Psychology Review, 7*(3), 313-322.

Torrance, E. P., Clements, C. B. & Goff, K. (1989). Mind-body learning among the elderly: Arts, fitness and incubation. *Educational Forum, 54*(1), 123-133.

Torrance, E. P. & Goff, K. (1989). A quiet revolution. *Journal of Creative Behavior, 23*(2), 136-145.

Torrance, E. P. & Goff, K. (1990). Fostering academic creativity in gifted students. *ERIC Digest, #E484.* Reston, VA: Council for Exceptional Children.

Torrance, E. P. & Goff, K. (1993). Expressive arts. In R. Kastenbaum (Ed.), *Encyclopedia of adult development* (p. 150-153). Phoenix, AZ: Orynx Press.

Torrance, E. P., Goff, K. & Satterfield, N. (1998). *Multicultural mentoring of the gifted and talented.* Waco, TX: Prufrock Press.

Torrance, E. P., Murdock, M. C. & Fletcher, D. (1996). *Creative problem solving through role playing.* Pretoria, South Africa: Benedic Books.

REFERENCES

Torrance, E. P. & Safter, H. T. (1990). *The incubation model of teaching: Getting beyond aha!* Buffalo, NY: Bearly Limited.

Torrance, E. P., Wu, T. H. & Ando, T. (1980). *Preliminary norms-technical manual: Demonstrator Torrance Tests of Creative Thinking.* Athens, GA: Georgia Studies of Creative Behavior, Athens, GA.

Vare, E. A. & Ptacek, G. (1987). *Mothers of invention.* NY: Quill.

Wallas, G. (1926). *The art of thought.* NY: Harcourt.

Williams, D. R. (1993). Cooperative learning and cultural diversity: Building caring communities in the cooperative classroom. In J. W. Putnam (Ed.), *Cooperative learning and strategies for inclusion: Celebrating diversity in the classroom* (p. 145-161). Baltimore: Paul H. Brookes.

Willard, R. D. (1977). Brease enlargement through visual imagery and hypnosis. *American journal of Clinical Hypnosis, 19,* 195-200.

Zdenek, M. (1983). *The right-brain experience.* NY: McGraw-Hill.

Ziv, A. (1980). Humor and creativity. *Creative Child and Adult Quarterly, 5*(3), 159-170.

Ziv, A. (1983). The influence of humorous atmoshpere on divergent thinking. *Contemporary Educational Psychology, 8,* 68-75.

SUBJECT INDEX

A
Adult, 4, 38-39, 49, 74, 77, 82, 116, 128, 129
  older, 128-132
Aging, 128-133
Art(s), 2, 73-80, 131
At-risk students, 125, 126, 155
Auditory learning, 30

B
Barriers to creativity, 38-39
Behavior, 5, 7, 12, 41, 42, 83
Brain, 31-34, 86
Brainstorming, 7, 14-17, 19, 104, 131, 133-134
  game, 133-134
  rules, 15

C
Change, 1, 3, 111, 129, 139, 141, 142, 143
Children, 5, 7, 13, 14, 25-42, 36-42, 52, 73, 74, 75, 77, 82, 125, 127
Classroom, 27, 34, 41, 113, 155

Clay activity, 20-22, 149-150
Collaborations, 59
Courage, 3, 5, 20, 49, 52, 62, 143
Cooperative learning, 26, 34-36
Creative
  abilities, 4, 11-24, 53, 82, 129
  expression, 2, 16, 74, 77, 78, 91
  learning, 2, 6, 25, 36-38, 41, 43-47, 82, 131
  personality, 1-2
  problem solving, 3, 4-5, 14, 41, 49, 59, 63-72
  problem solving model, 65-67
  process, 1-4, 12, 36, 43, 44, 45, 79, 81
  talents, 41, 127
  thinking, 1, 2, 4, 5, 12-13, 25, 44, 65, 83, 129, 133
Creativity
  definition, 2-3, 11-13, 25

research, 1-9, 11-13, 74, 93, 131-133
tests, 3-4, 7, 13, 24, 28
tips, 137-146
Cultural diversity, 4, 7, 26, 27, 34, 35
Curiosity, 25-26, 38, 39, 45, 111

D
Dance, 41, 131
Drama, 131

E
Education, 4, 34, 37, 62, 77, 93
ElderHostel, 130
Elaboration, 13, 22-24, 60
Environment, 1-2, 12, 27, 29, 34, 35, 44, 45, 47, 61, 78, 128
Evaluation, 15, 41
Experimental learning, 25, 73, 116

F
Family, 41-42, 94, 106, 107, 122-123
mentors,
Fantasy, 37, 39, 82
Fear of failure, 55-56
Female inventors, 94-100

Fitness, 131
Flexibility, 13, 17-19, 60, 77, 83, 132, 133, 137, 143-144
Fluency, 13-17, 60, 132, 133
Future, 4, 14, 18, 35, 67, 81, 90, 91, 94, 111-114
instructional strategies, 112-114
Future problem solving program, 67
Futuristics, 111-112

G
Game, 100, 134
Game activity,
Game inventing,
Gender, 7, 27-29, 93
Gifted, 4, 5, 6, 7, 8, 9
Goose story, 60-61
Grandparents, 41-42, 125
Group activities, 26, 75, 83, 148-150
Group problem solving, 26, 35
Guardians, 41-42
Guidance, 121

SUBJECT INDEX

H
Health, 2, 51, 61-62, 75, 76, 83-88, 91, 115, 132, 154
Hemispericity, 31-34
Humor, 75, 82-84, 90

I
Ideas, 3, 14, 19, 20, 23, 38, 100-103, 107, 148-150
Imagery, 20-22, 88-90, 154
Imagination, 1, 12, 15, 37-38, 43, 65, 75, 81, 89, 110, 114, 117, 133, 138, 141-142, 152
Incubation, 2, 7, 43-47
Incubation model of teaching, 20-22, 45-47, 131, 133, 152-155
activities,
Insights, 6-7
Intelligence(s), 4, 29-30, 49, 50
Interdependence, 9, 27, 35
Inventing, 93-114
activities,
tidbits, 107-111
Inventors, 27
IQ tests, 4, 28, 49

K
Kinesthetic learning, 30-31

L
Laughter,
Learners, 16, 18, 26-28, 30-31, 35, 36, 42, 44-45, 100
Learning, 35-42, 43-47
auditory, 30
cooperative, 34-36
creative, 2, 6
independent,
kinesthetic, 30-31
self-initiated,
sensory, 29-31
skills, 82
styles, 14, 28, 29
supportive environment, 2
visual, 30
Leisure, 127-128
Lifelong creativity, 127-135
LifeSlider, 105-106
Life satisfaction, 128-133

M
Manifestor for Children, 9
Maslow, A. H., 50-53, 61-62, 73, 82

Mentor(s), 4, 6, 9, 94,
    115-126, 131
  guidelines, 117-120
  programs, 124
Mentoring, 115-126
  gender differences,
    123-124
Motivation, 14, 45, 91
Multiple intelligences,
  24-30
Music, 29, 143

N
Negotiation, 7, 117
Neurolingquistic
  programming, 30-31
Nontraditional learn-
  ing, 8

O
Older adults,
Originality, 13, 19-22,
  60, 133

P
Painting activity, 150
Parental strengths,
  56-58
  survey results, 58
Parents, 14, 41-42,
  56-58, 123, 127
Peaceful Hideaway,
  152-154

Personal strengths,
  53-56
Placebos, 86-87
Play dough recipe, 149
Proactive, 63
Prototype, 101-102,
  104, 105
Provocative questions,
  18-19

Q
Quality of Life Program,
  131-132
Questioning, 18-19, 36,
  38, 41, 137, 139-140

R
Recyclables, 68-72
Recycling, 67-72
Relaxation, 43, 144, 154
  activity, 20-22
Retirement, 125,
  127-135

S
Scamper technique,
  17-18
School(s), 24, 27, 29,
  34, 42, 73, 125, 141
Self-actualization,
  50-53, 73, 90, 133,
  134
  determination,
  discipline, 1, 12, 63

SUBJECT INDEX

discovery, 1, 12, 63, 154
esteem, 34
reliance,
Senior Savvy Brainstormers, 134
Senses, 11, 25, 29-31, 36, 74, 78, 88, 142
Sensory learning, 29-31, 74
Singing, 41
Sociodrama, 113-114
split-brain studies, 31-33
Storytelling, 23, 41
Strengths, 5, 7, 9, 14, 20, 24, 26, 27, 35, 53-62, 82, 129, 144
Stress, 41, 82, 88
Survival training, 11-12

T

Teachers, 6, 9, 14, 26, 27, 40-41, 44-45, 127
The Creativity Association for Women, 103-104
Torrance, E. P., 1-9, 11-13, 19-20, 22-23, 24, 25, 27, 28, 37, 38, 44, 63, 66, 67, 74, 75, 81, 82, 86, 93, 111-114, 116, 123, 124, 131, 132
insights, 7

Truth, 45
Turtle Shells, 106-107

V

Visual learning, 30
Visualization, 20-22, 43, 152, 154

W

Warm-up, 20, 45-46, 47, 152, 155
Wellness, 81-91
Women, 27-29, 94-100, 103-107
Wonder, 37, 62
World Future Society, 114